Hiking
South Korea

Hiking
South Korea

88 Day Hikes from Sandy Beaches to Rocky Peaks

Production Management: Amy Reed & Saeah Wood
Art Direction: Saeah Wood
Cover Design & Layout: Ivica Jandrijevic
Editorial: Amy Reed & Christa Evans
Map Illustration: Jasna Cizler
Design & Editorial Support: Elizabeth Evey & Bridget Manzella

ISBN:
Paperback: 978-1-955671-24-8
E-Book: 978-1-955671-25-5

otterpine.com

Photo Credits:

Unless noted below, the images in this book were photographed and provided by the author.

The publisher would like to thank the following for their permission to reproduce their photographs:

Stock.adobe.com: Tawatchai1990 **front cover, i, iv;** Joseph **vii;** Tatiana Grozetskaya **ix;** Atakorn **1;** Boonkerd **5;** Sangoh **9, 70, 144;** FornStudio **13;** Bennytrapp **14;** Natalya **15;** Photo203 **15;** Mr.wijit amkapet **21;** Sigint **29;** Chanchai **38, 57;** Sanga **front flap, 42, 60, 87, 125;** Mongkol **front flap, 44;** Daewan **58;** SiHo **64;** Bardia **front flap, 65;** MarsiWWW **74;** CJ Nattanai **77;** Nathan **85;** Joshua Davenport **88;** 문구 강 **89;** Dudlajzov **91;** Lhboucault **91;** Michele Burgess **93;** Shoenberg3 **94;** YOUSUK **98;** Nathan **99;** Aaron90311 **101, 119;** photo_HYANG **103, 104;** Jipen **105;** Nogravityphoto **107;** Kalyakan **107;** Dsfagqe **110;** 21pro **110;** Thomas Oliver/ Wirestock **115;** Shin sangwoon **118, 179;** Kingjung **81;** Wirestock Exclusives **124;** Barbarico **126;** Aerrant **127;** Dudlajzov **127;** Yeonghason **131;** Restuccia Giancarlo **140;** Hecke71 **148;** 隼人 岩崎 **149;** Homank76 **back flap, 155;** Kamchai **162, 178;** Eqroy **181;** Korkeng **221;** Deb_NSWP **234;** Kit Leong **241.**

Dreamstime.com: Jonkio4 **128.**

Freepik.com: Gorkhe1980 **68.**

Shutterstock.com: Panwasin seemala **7, 114, 167;** Janine Muenger **59;** Seo Sang Jin **108;** Sangoh Bae **109, 134;** Stock for you **131;** Yeongsik Im **142.**

Contents

Acknowledgments

This book would not have been possible without the kindness and generosity of many, many people. In particular, I would like to thank TaeSung Lee, DongSuk Seo, JooHyun Kyung, MinWoo Kim, Peter Broad, Paul Ware, Brett Sheridan, Dave and Julene Messineo, Petya Filipova, David and Elizabeth Moras, Bob Hayhoe, Mike Murphy, Adam and Diana Collins, Edward Rademaker, Nicholas Kauffman, John and Sarah Sicinski, and Daryl Attwood. I am indebted forever for your

kindness and enthusiasm and for your generous contribution of resources, skills, and knowledge. Thank you for your support and friendship.

I must also thank my darling daughters—Vivienne, Karoline, Viktoria, and Kaitlynn—who taught me to see the outdoors through the eyes of children, full of fun and wonder.

My loving wife Jozefina has provided me with many, many hours of peace in which to write, edit, and research in a near-constant swirl of challenges over the past 5 years, including job loss, financial hardship, moving abroad, selling our home, and homeschooling our children. She has shielded me from the very real day-to-day toils and worries of raising four young children so I could complete this book. Thank you, my love, for everything.

Finally, a big thank you to my parents who taught me at an early age that things are generally hard and that nothing worth doing ever comes easy or quick. It's because of this training early on in life that I was able to persevere.

Preface

My interest in hiking began the year I was unexpectedly deployed to Korea.

I vividly remember the day I received the phone call from my then-employer's New York office letting me know I was going to Korea, not Denmark. I had just come in from cutting the grass on a hot summer afternoon. I remember the iced tea: it was in a large glass and very sweet. Of course, I didn't have a coaster—a habit that perturbed my mother to no end.

The call went like this: "Hi Erik, you're not going to Denmark anymore. Instead, you're being sent to a place that needs extra manpower. It's called Okpo. I don't know where that is, but I do know you need shots before going there, so please come to New York." I recall asking about my prized possessions, which at the age of 24 consisted of two used cardboard boxes of marine engineering textbooks, a few foreign postcards, some dirty boilersuits, and a calculator, all of which had already been shipped to Denmark. I was told they were on their way to Korea.

With an arm full of shots and a yellow WHO vaccination card to prove it, I found myself a week later in the last days of summer in 1995, in transit from New York to Korea on a nearly empty Northwest Airlines flight. It soon started to fill up with US Army soldiers getting ready for a deployment to Korea. We stopped in Anchorage, Alaska to refuel, and nearly everyone deplaned there except for the soldiers. Another 12 hours passed, and then I was in the backseat of a taxi, driving from Pusan Airport through unfamiliar towns and cities until, 2 ½ hours later, we reached a small, two-lane bridge.

It was late, and I awoke to see it was dark and drizzling. A policeman was checking driver's licenses and registrations, and behind him, a soldier with a rifle stood half-concealed behind a pile of sandbags. We crossed the bridge of rough, deeply-grooved asphalt, finally arriving on Geoje—what many call "Fantasy Island." From there, we passed darkened buildings, many workshops, and a few small cranes, everything dimly lit. After climbing a hill, the village of Okpo came into view.

The days and weeks that followed were the usual whirlwind of shipyard life, PPE, visits to key stakeholders, surveys in the shipyard, union strike activities, and the general industriousness and seriousness imparted by Koreans in almost everything that happens—with a dose of chaos thrown in for good measure. In the evenings, after work, I wandered into bars and raw seafood restaurants with colleagues from a dozen nations. Soon, however, I was mostly staying in with bowl of spicy instant noodles (sometimes two), watching Star TV.

Something was missing. It kept calling out to me, from the deck of a ship, from the parking lot, when I was often soaked in sweat and covered in insulation and blasting grit. I would take a break and look across the dust, the motion, and the chaos to the verdant green hills all around the bay and to a pointy little rock outcrop near the top of one hill in particular.

Eventually, I found a fellow who was nice enough to show me the way to the top of that hill, and those first few steps into the forest have led to a lifelong love of all things natural, with hiking at its core. And so it began, a love affair that continues to this day.

Not long after that first trek up the hill, I was introduced to The Hash House Harriers (HHH) on Geoje Island, an organization that calls itself as a "drinking club with a running problem." It is a long-standing group on the island (and a global organization as well) that since 1981 has been led progressively by senior volunteer "Hares." It was through the HHHs that I first encountered the mountains of Korea. I fondly remember my initiation ceremony after my third hashing event (drinking far too much beer, far too fast, from a sweaty boot—not mine), followed with the singing and "naming ceremony" (a name which is not to be repeated here!).

Regardless, I am pleased to report that the Geoje HHH is alive and well, and "Hashes" are set biweekly with notice given at the Geoje Foreign Residents Association (GFRA) clubhouse. It's a great way to build friendships, get exercise, and see some of the island too. As the island has gentrified and become more attractive over the years for families, many of the HHH events have also become family friendly, although some remain the purview of the "old guard and old ways."

Those first hikes on Geoje awakened a love of hiking that brought me to the mountains of mainland Korea, where over the next several years I continued to explore on my own, with friends and other Harriers, and eventually, with my wife and daughters. I hope your hiking adventures in South Korea bring you the same joy that mine have brought my family and me.

Introduction

Few things in life are as humble as taking a walk. By the age of one, most of us have mastered it in one form or another, and yet in adulthood we spend far too little time walking and far too much in a stationary or moving seat, glued to a computer, a TV, or a steering wheel.

You have probably heard that you should exercise daily, but for most people, working out is just another chore, just another item to scratch off a long to-do list. If, like most people, you work in an office or any other indoor setting, you probably know the pain of spending even more of your limited free time inside a gym. If you have kids, it gets even harder, since you're not just taking away from time outside but also time you could be spending with your family.

Yet, a simple solution remains: you can always take a walk.

Walking can be done by people of all ages and abilities. One only needs to slip on a comfortable pair of shoes, sling on a daypack, and step onto the sidewalk or into the nearby woods. If you can invest more time and energy, you can try getting out to those nearby "high places." Regardless of the weather, a day spent walking, especially with family and friends, is always a good day.

This guide is intended for everyone: for the serious hikers among us, for people who enjoy leisurely strolls, and for families with young kids. Part I provides helpful information about both hiking in Korea and hiking in general.

In researching and composing this book, I collected free handouts (from park rangers, temple monks, and tourist information centers), filled several notebooks (with scribbled notes, sketches, and rubbings), and took thousands of photos. I then spent countless hours poring over this raw material to select what would be most helpful for the average reader looking to explore mainland South Korea and Geoje Island. While many people may be most familiar with the capital city of Seoul and the northern regions of South Korea, I have chosen to focus heavily on the southern area of the mainland and the island of Geoje because these are the areas closest to my heart and, quite frankly, they are the areas I know the best.

In Part II and III of the book, I have organized the hikes first by geographical region (with color-coded tabs assigned to each), and then by level of difficulty—providing clear directions, maps, descriptions, and important details for each one.

Whether you want to push a stroller along a paved path under some cherry trees, or ascend a near-vertical, ice-encrusted granite monolith at -28 degrees Celsius, Korea offers it all in terms of hiking. For those in the middle of these two extremes—the "everyman," the amateur naturalist, or amateur hiker—South Korea offers a wide variety of escapes to commune with nature in peace and safety. It is my sincere hope that these pages will give you the tools and guidance you need to explore the many wonderful hikes of mainland South Korea and Geoje Island. So slip on a pair of boots, sling a pack over your shoulder, and hit the trail!

Part I

The Basics

 # Beautiful Korea

The Korean Peninsula is a most beguiling place. You have an Organization for Economic Co-operation and Development (OECD) world leader in advanced technology exporting globally to the south of the Demilitarized Zone (DMZ), while a nearly closed hermit kingdom lies to the north, secured by staunch Communist-era ideology, threatening to unleash a "sea of fire" by nuclear bombardment at a moment's notice, or so the threats go. Meanwhile, life goes on for the 75 million people who call the Korean Peninsula home, two-thirds of them in the south and a third in the north.

A common people united by language, literature, over 5,000 years of history and common traditions, while divided by pretty much everything else since 1945, Koreans live with the legacy of both World War II and the Cold War era, while striving to find a peaceful way forward, together or apart.

One aspect of the Korean Peninsula that transcends the political issues of the day and underlies this book is the true natural beauty of the land itself. Looking beyond the vast cities, huge industrial complexes, modern motorways, and high-speed KTX railway, Korea is an astoundingly beautiful place, covered in rugged mountains, verdant valleys, wave-lashed cliffs, and white, sandy beaches. Korea is a nature lover's paradise.

Yet, Korea is not an especially well-known destination on the international hiking circuits. Japan, Nepal, New Zealand, and others attract many more travelers to their lofty peaks and windswept trails. This is a real shame, however, for in the mountains of Korea, one can find true solace for the mind, body, and soul.

High up in the craggy peaks lie small hermitage temples, age-old wind chimes, and rustling bamboo groves. Farther down the slopes, the massive temple complexes dot the valleys, surrounded by rice paddies and fields of Korean spicy red pepper plants. Meanwhile, the springs flow, the creeks fill, and the waterfalls tumble over the granite outcrops to a network of rivers far below. Among all the beauty, the seasons play out their time-honored cycle: from green-covered slopes of summer, abuzz with wildlife; to the kaleidoscope of colors in autumn; to the crisp, clear skies of winter, with the crunch of snow underfoot; followed by the rebirth of springtime's fields and hills, practically exploding with wildflowers and butterflies. Be warned: Korea will captivate you with her beauty, and once bitten, you will want to come back again and again.

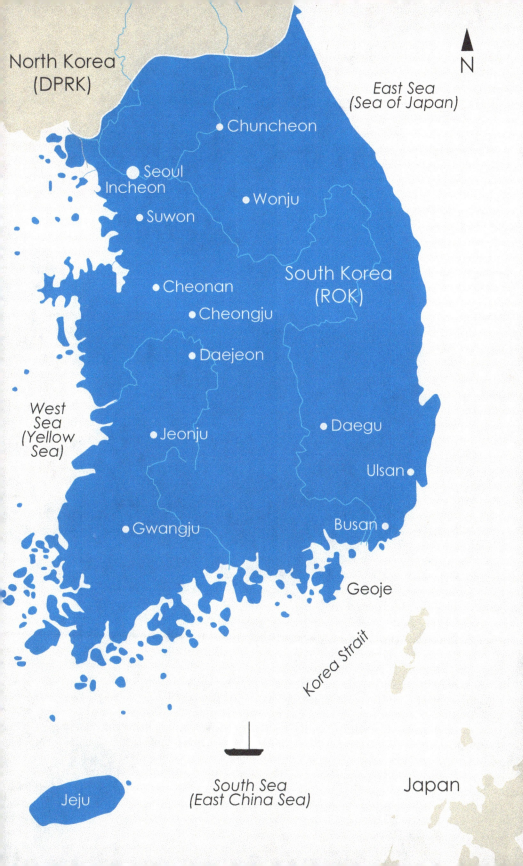

Geoje Island

Geoje Island (or Geoje-do) is just off the southwestern coast of the port city of Busan. The second-largest island in Korea (after Jeju), Geoje encompasses 383 square kilometers and is blessed with numerous mountains, including the "11 Famous Peaks" (or 12 depending on who you speak to). Having hiked all of them a number of times, and many smaller ones as well, I lean in support of the 11 Famous Peaks of Geoje (all of which you will find in this book).

Most of the mountains on Geoje are rather steep and are guaranteed to get the heart racing in the first 5 minutes, but the highest elevation on the island is found at the top of Garasan (at 585 meters) in the far south. One amazing aspect of all the mountains on the island is that there are beautiful views out to sea from every one of them. Many of Geoje's bays, as well as the surrounding islands, are visible from mountain heights. On clear days, you might even see as far as Japan's Tsushima Island (60 kilometers to the southeast of the island).

The waters around Geoje are not as heavily polluted as you may think, given that two of the world's largest shipyards call the island home. In fact, the opposite is the case. The water is clean and fully accessible for swimming and water sports. The waters around Geoje are also full of fish and shellfish, and many aquaculture farms (for growing oysters especially) are also located there. The beaches of Geoje are wonderful for day use or overnight camping. I highly recommend the experience of sitting around a roaring fire with friends, with otherworldly views of the mountains and the sea.

Geoje Island is home to Daewoo Shipbuilding and Marine Engineering (DSME) and Samsung Heavy Industries (SHI). These two shipyards are among a small number of the world's largest marine construction yards, second only to Hyundai Heavy Industries (HHI) in Ulsan on the Korean East Sea coastline, north of Pusan and south of Pohang.

However, the long-term commercial viability of heavy industry on the island is under constant review in light of intense international (namely Chinese) competition in the sector. Geoje City, rebranded the "Blue City", and the provincial government are actively working to develop the appeal and infrastructure of Geoje Island as a leading tourist destination.

After 6 years of construction, the 8.2-kilometer Geoga (Geoje) Grand Bridge (including a 3.7-kilometer undersea tunnel) opened in 2010. The bridge reduced travel time between Geoje Island and Busan from 3 hours to less than

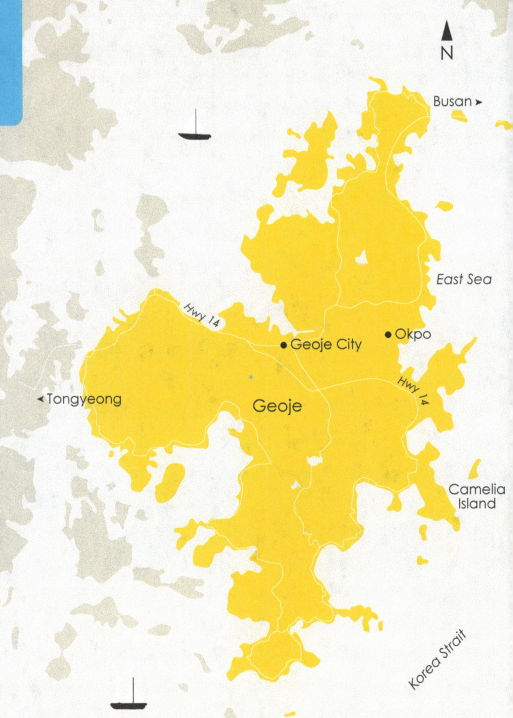

N

Busan ➤

East Sea

Hwy 14

● Geoje City   ● Okpo

◄ Tongyeong

Hwy 14

Geoje

Camelia
Island

Korea Strait

1 hour. The bridge has had an enormous impact on the island in terms of rapid investment and development of tourism based on second home ownership and pension rentals, the development of which is evident all over the island. The bridge has also made life much more enjoyable for the local Korean and expatriate residents. Day trips can now be easily made to Busan for shopping and leisure activities, including hiking on the mainland!

With a total population of over 240,000 people, Geoje will have upwards of 3,000–6,000 expatriate residents at any given time, primarily engaged by foreign shipowners, class societies, or equipment manufacturers. Over 60–80 nationalities are represented on the island, either long-term residents or transient workers. Geoje Island is uniquely diverse, and this makes it an interesting place to live, work, or visit.

These days, quality supermarkets and coffeehouses exist in abundance on Geoje Island, so there is no need to go off island for Western staples. Back in the day,

however, buying a loaf of bread or slice of cheese involved an arduous hour-long trip by ferryboat (and then by taxi) to a specialty store of a large five-star hotel in Busan, or a 3-hour (one-way) car trip. This changed in the 1980s, when the Geoje Foreign Residents Association (GFRA) was established as a club where resident expatriates could gather for a drink (or two) and enjoy a meal and a game of pool in a Western pub-like atmosphere.

The GFRA was once the island's "hub" and a true home away from home for expatriates. Today, you can look at the GFRA blackboard, just behind the pool table, at decades upon decades of long-retired ship surveyors and their families, all smiling and standing in various groupings with interesting names appended, some family friendly (but most not).

While the island is relatively small in size, its beauty and concentration of great hikes is unparalleled. It is worth a special trip from the mainland for anyone interested in experiencing all the best that Korea can offer.

 # What to Expect on the Trail

The Trails

The most difficult thing about a hike in Korea is oftentimes just finding the trailhead. For this reason, I have made sure to provide clear GPS coordinates matching the location of each trailhead in this guidebook. Since hiking is such a popular pastime in Korea, the trails are usually well maintained. Trail conditions are generally very good in national parks and vary between fair to good in provincial and locally maintained parks. Features like small bridges, ladders and stairs, ropes, and chains facilitate safer and easier hiking. Due to high usage and many keen Korean hikers, you will never be alone for long on the trail, and if confused or lost, a smile and request for help will usually result in a form of trail language and a hand-drawn map that will get you headed in the right direction. However, one should always carry a copy of a good map (and this guide) to assist in navigating the route.

Trail Signs and Trail Markers

Most trailheads and junctions will have clear trail signs in Hangul and English (always in national parks, and sporadically in other places) and will provide distances in kilometers or meters to summits, temples, shelters, and similar

important waypoints. In Korea, it's typical to encounter both these official trail signs as well as various kinds of trail markers such as rock cairns, flags, and stone stele-type markers placed by other hikers. You will find these kinds of handmade markers near summits in particular.

Temples, Shrines, and Hermitages

Buddhism was introduced to Korea by China in AD 372. All across the country, you will find both sprawling complexes of the main orders and smaller satellite

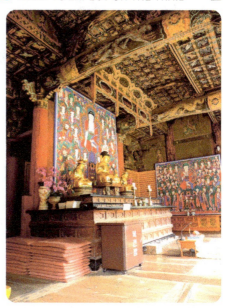

temples, as well as hermitage temples far up in the mountains. Near hermitage temples, it is common to find Buddhist shrines inside caves. Many of the temple sites are between 500 and 1,500 years old. Unfortunately, during the Japanese Invasions (Imjin War) of the 1590s up through the more recent Korean War (1950–1953), the majority of the temples were heavily damaged or outright destroyed. Fortunately, the Korean people have rebuilt (in many cases following the original design and using traditional

methods) these cultural and religious heritage sites. Thus, while the wooden structures themselves are typically modern reconstructions, the stone foundations are often original.

Many of the hikes in this book include a visit to nearby temples. I have always reveled in the beauty and peace of these sites. Often located at the head of a valley or on a watercourse of some kind, these sacred places are capable of transporting you back to a less hurried time, far from the hustle and bustle of modern ways. Here you can smell the incense and listen to monks reciting the sutras and playing wooden instruments. I have found a sense of inner well-being from these experiences, and I surely hope you will be able to as well. I encourage you take your shoes off, sit in the back of a temple, close your eyes, and maybe even try to meditate.

Korean Hiking Clubs

It would be remiss not to mention the other important trail marker in use all across Korea: hiking club pennant flags. These colorful strips made of a combination of fabric and plastic come

in all manner of bright colors and are usually covered in the names of clubs and events. These flags are placed on branches and the like all along the trails, especially at key junctions or in places where a common mistake could be made. If in doubt, or feeling a bit lost, these flags indicate you are on the right trail. These flags should be respected, in addition to the other trail markers.

Transportation

Korea is a very modern country, and many forms of public transportation exist in the cities. On Geoje Island, however, public transport isn't always available. Due to the small (sometimes one-way) access roads at trailheads, or lack of nearby bus stops or similar, the only method for transport is a private car (or a chartered bus for larger groups). Fortunately, cars are plentiful and GPS coverage is excellent across Korea, so it is easy to know where you are and where you need to go.

Trail Culture in Korea

You can expect to encounter friendly, happy, and generous people on the trail. As a foreigner hiking in Korea, you will be warmly greeted and may also be invited for some rice wine and a seemingly unending buffet of sensationally good (albeit spicy) food! Go easy on the rice wine (and soju) if you have a long way to go. It can pack a punch!

Dos and Don'ts

Nature is to be enjoyed by everyone. We share it with those on the path, and what we leave behind affects those who follow in our footsteps. Korea has set aside 22 national parks to protect mountain, coastal, and cultural treasures. Additionally, there are provincial parks and many locally maintained parks/trails throughout the country, including on Geoje Island. It is important to remember to limit noise from electronic devices and to "take only pictures and leave only footsteps." All trash is to be packed out and disposed of properly ("leave no trace"). Finally, avoid fires, especially in the dry season from October to April when forests can be tinder dry and covered with fuel in the form of leaves and wood detritus just ready to burn.

Nearly everyone in Korea has a smartphone, and the use of smartphones to take pictures is commonplace. That being said, the rules of ethical photography should always be followed. Always get approval before taking someone's picture. Also, be cognizant that taking pictures of modified mountaintops, industrial facilities, transport/power infrastructure, or other nontouristic features is frowned upon and/or strictly forbidden because such locations may have a military use or connection. Be respectful and do not photograph these things, for everyone's sake.

Finally, do be curious, be friendly, and don't be scared. South Korea is one of the safest countries in the world. The Koreans are hardworking, hard playing, and a truly honest and friendly people. A simple "Hello!" ("annyeonghaseyo;" 안녕하세) spoken on the trail will instantly bring smiles and camaraderie Make sure you do it frequently and loudly, with confidence, sincerity, and a big smile to account for your poor pronunciation and horrible accent! The other excellent phrase to know and use frequently is "Thank you," or "gomabseubnida" (고맙습니다). Make sure you thank people for stepping aside, for offering a bite to eat, for anything... you can never say "thank you" enough in any language! For more Korean phrases that are useful on the trail please see the glossary on page 254.

Food and Drink
Korean cuisine is world famous, and for good reason: it's both healthy and delicious! On the trail, you will find many Koreans hiking with friends or colleagues from work, school, or church.

Some of these clubs will be very organized and sometimes bring gas stoves to heat up elaborate meals with an array of side dishes, including the essential kimchee, and desserts like sweet rice cakes filled with red bean paste. All of this is commonly washed down with cool makkoli rice wine, soju, or beer (or all three!). Feasts like this are commonplace on the trail in Korea. And if you come across such a group happily eating and joking, don't be surprised if you are invited to join in. If you can, I encourage you to do this at least once.

For more routine hiking, common fare consisting of water and nonperishable high-energy snacks are recommended and may be found everywhere, including motorway rest areas across the country. Items such as chocolate, dried fruit, nuts, and crackers are all popular hiking foods that offer a lot of nourishment and energy but are still relatively lightweight.

Mountain Bikes
In some cases, popular trails on Geoje Island are split on the steep downhill sections so that mountain bikers (MTB) and hikers do not share the same trails. This is moderately effective, and care must always be taken when on the trail to avoid a rather nasty surprise for both parties. Fortunately, the occurrence of such incidents remains low.

Safety and Preparation

Disclaimer

Hiking is a fun and enjoyable pastime, but as with any outdoor activity, it comes with inherent risks. It is important that those who wish to use this guide take their experience and fitness level into consideration. Although I have made every attempt to provide timely and accurate information in this guide, things do change from time to time. It is up to you to ensure you have the right gear and are adequately prepared for the weather and current trail conditions. If something doesn't feel right one day, then give it a miss and come back another time. The mountains were here before us, and they will be there after us, too—so you have time, don't worry.

In summary, hike at your own risk. (Please see the Limit of Liability statement on copyright page.)

Insects and Wildlife

Snakes

Snakes reside across Korea, including Geoje Island. They are most active in the late spring through early fall. You typically won't encounter them in the colder months when the land is covered with snow and ice. Please follow these standard recommendations that apply anywhere in the world that snakes may be encountered.

Do not place your hands or feet in dark places. Snakes can often be found hiding under rocks, especially alongside streams. Generally speaking, it is always a good idea to stay on the trail and stay out of high grasses and bushes. When walking, make sure to look where you are going and occasionally stomp the ground to alert snakes of your presence, allowing them to depart from your path before you even see them (most of the time). Wear sturdy footwear that protects your feet and ankles. Please, no open-toed shoes or hiking sandals! If you do encounter a snake, back carefully away from it and pass it with a wide margin. Fortunately, snakes are not overly aggressive in Korea, but they can strike if surprised or threatened.

There are three main varieties of venomous pit vipers in Korea and one variety of tiger snake. These snakes, and in fact, all venomous snakes the

world over, can typically be identified by their triangular-shaped heads. A more rounded head indicates a nonvenomous snake species. In the rare case of a snake bite, first calm the victim, apply a pressure-type bandage to the whole limb affected, immobilize the limb with a splint, and then move the victim to the closest medical care facility. If possible, try to obtain a photo of the snake to help the medical staff identify the snake to assist in treatment.

Korea is NOT Australia or Africa. Over the past 20 years, while hiking in Korea, I have only encountered snakes on four or five occasions, and none of them were venomous. So relax and take the necessary precautions, and everything will be just fine!

Ticks, Centipedes, and Mosquitoes

Ticks, centipedes, and mosquitoes are all present in the Republic of Korea (ROK). On Geoje, most of these insects will be prevalent from March through November due to its warmer and moister maritime climate. Use mosquito repellent with at least 20–30 percent DEET, applying it to your pack and clothing only. Unless it is excessively hot, cover up with clothing, hats, and close-toed shoes. The less you expose your skin, the less insects will be able to bite you. It is also very advisable that you obtain a vaccination for Japanese encephalitis as well, a common mosquito-borne illness prevalent in Northeast Asia. Fortunately, this vaccine is widely available at clinics in Korea and is very inexpensive.

Tick and centipede bites can cause serious illness, especially in children. You won't necessarily feel the tick bite, but you will have a sharp burning pain from a centipede bite almost immediately. Both of these are pests on the trail, but in my mind, at least the centipede plays fair: if it bites, you probably stepped on it or

otherwise scared it, and it is acting in self-defense (similar to a snake). For most people, a centipede bite will be painful and cause swelling, but it won't cause serious damage. However, if a person has an allergy to centipede venom (similar to allergies to bee stings), it can cause a severe allergic reaction, even anaphylaxis in very rare cases.

Ticks, however, are indiscriminate, hard to see or feel, and hard to avoid. In general, stay on the trail and avoid tall grass and bushes. Also avoid animals such as dogs and cats as well as wildlife that may be carriers. Tuck your pants into your socks or wear leggings to limit access to other parts of your body. Following every hike, do a self-inspection. Check the scalp, behind/in the ears, under the armpits, in the groin, and behind the knees and between the toes. If you do find a tick, don't panic. Try to remove it by pulling steadily and gently with tweezers from the head (not stomach) until the tick is fully removed from the skin. Dispose of the tick properly so it cannot bite anyone else. Clean the affected area with soap

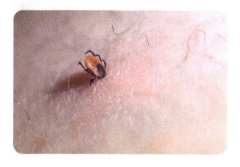

and water and watch for any unusual redness or swelling; if that occurs, visit your doctor.

Like mosquitoes, ticks carry diseases. While Lyme disease does exist in Korea, it is not as prevalent as it is in the US. Of more concern is Severe Fever Thrombocytopenia Syndrome (SFTS), which was first identified in Korea in 2013. It is prevalent in Northeast Asia and found in Northeast China and all of Japan as well. Symptoms of SFTS include fever, headaches, muscle and joint pain, dizziness, and tiredness, then after 3–7 days, patients may develop bruise-like rashes in the mouth and on the skin, followed by liver and kidney ailments. In some rare cases, the disease may cause other complications and could lead to death. If any of these symptoms occur after a tick bite, it is very important to visit a medical facility for treatment.

Bears and Boars

Long ago, the Korean Peninsula (as with much of the world) teemed with large and small game. Then humans came, and over the millennia, our hunter-gatherer ancestors reduced the animal populations and our planet's biodiversity along with it. Add in several wars, famines, and agricultural and urban development, and you have today's world, where many of

the large land animals that once roamed the Earth freely are contained within zoos and preserves. Korea has suffered this fate along with many other developed nations.

In an effort to rebuild native animal populations in Korea, the Korea National Park Service (KNPS) has supported the reintroduction of bears into select areas in the national parks. Jirisan National Park, among others, now supports small populations of bears. Accordingly, the KNPS wants visitors to be aware of this activity and has set up warning posters in the vicinity of bear habitats. To my knowledge there have been no negative bear-human contacts to date, and it's very unlikely that you will see a bear as they quite understandably want to avoid us.

When on the trail, if you believe that you may be close to a bear, it's best to make a lot of noise so that it has time to move away from you. If you happen to encounter a bear, make yourself look large in addition to making noise, and this will usually scare the animal away. That said, the risk of a bear attack in Korea is virtually nonexistent.

More common than bears are wild boars. They roam the forests and mountainsides and are increasingly coming into villages and cities looking for food, especially in autumn and winter. In recent news, the deadly African swine fever (ASF) virus has been detected in dead wild hogs found near the inter-Korean border. Wild boars can be aggressive, so the best thing to do if you see one on a hike is to avoid it. If you find yourself close to one, back away slowly (do not run or turn your back on it), and if possible, try to reach higher ground.

Weather Considerations

No matter what season you're hiking in, always check the weather before hitting the trail, and make sure you're prepared with the proper clothing and gear.

A Norwegian friend of mine once told me, "There is no such thing as bad weather, only bad clothing." I believe this is true. Buy reliable gear from reputable retailers and top brands. You will thankful you did if you ever get caught in bad weather!

Summer

Hiking in Korea can be enjoyed year-round However, fall through spring are preferable to summer, given the high humidity and temperatures (24–38 degrees Celsius). If you do go hiking in the summer, it's best to hit the trails in the morning, before the heat and humidity make it unbearable. A nice hike at 5:30 or 6:00 a.m. is a great way to start the day. You'll enjoy the peace on the trail (while everyone else is asleep) and will hopefully catch a glorious sunrise. Later in the afternoon, especially in July and August, violent thunderstorms are prevalent, and it's best not to be on the slopes due to the potential for lightning and heavy rain. One highlight in the summer is camping, however. Beach camping is very

popular on Geoje and well worth a try! Finally, typhoon season runs from June to November, and heavy rains, flooding, and high winds impact Korea during this time. Always check the weather forecast before heading out.

Fall

Autumn in Korea arrives with clearing skies, colorful leaves, and relief from the high humidity and oppressive heat of the summer. This is the most popular season for hiking across Korea. Brightly colored hiking paraphernalia will be on full display all over the country as trails become clogged with hikers wearing every shade of neon. Meanwhile, leaf peepers lugging around camera gear jostle with hikers in order to get the best photos of the brightly colored leaves. Average temperatures for this season will be 10–21 degrees Celsius.

Winter

Winter temperatures in Korea can plunge below -20 to -30 degrees Celsius, and there can be a lot of snow in the mountains. Make sure to check the forecast, call ahead to national parks, and be "situationally aware." Geoje Island has mild winters compared to peninsular Korea. Daily temperatures in December through February will be approximately -2 to 10 degrees Celsius, and conditions will oftentimes be crystal clear. Winter is

one of my favorite times to go hiking as there are no bugs, and great views abound from the trails atop the peaks and ridges since much of the foliage has fallen away. It's common to encounter a little frost above 500 meters on the peaks of Geoje, but this will not usually last more than a day or two. Note that snow is rather rare on Geoje, but it does occur at times.

Spring

The flowers are in bloom at this time of year, and on sunny days, Korea is ablaze with color! Average temperatures are 8–22 degrees Celsius. The rains return, and so does the Huang Sa—the "yellow dust" that is carried by the jet stream from the Gobi Desert in northern China and Mongolia. This, coupled with the pollen from the forests, covers everything with a fine yellow layer of dust. The Korea Meteorological Association (KMA) website provides daily forecasts for the dust/haze, with associated warnings when air quality is poor. On such days it's better to skip the hiking and plan for your next trip.

Exposure
There are very real dangers associated with being underprepared for the weather: hypothermia in winter, heat exhaustion/sunstroke in summer, and dehydration at any time of the year.

Hypothermia will be most prevalent during the winter, but if inadequately clothed and without shelter and warmth, it is possible to experience hypothermia any time of the year, especially at higher elevations. The best way to avoid hypothermia is to have the right gear, the right physical conditioning, warm liquids, and a backup plan that includes knowledge of shelter locations nearby. Additionally, apply the buddy system on the trail. This will help to ensure that everyone looks after one another and can act right away if anyone in the group shows symptoms of hypothermia. Early symptoms will include a general withdrawal from talking, a slower pace on the trail with more stumbling, numbing in the extremities and loss of dexterity, and confused thoughts and speech. If these symptoms occur, make sure to get the person affected to a shelter with warmth right away. Monitor them closely while providing warm liquids until the symptoms subside.

Heat exhaustion and heatstroke typically occur during the hottest months of the year when the body becomes unable to maintain its normal temperature due to exposure to direct sun and heat, usually coupled with dehydration. At the onset of symptoms, it is important to take immediate action, which includes stopping the activity at hand, providing water, and taking a rest in the shade. Use a fan or wet cloths to produce an additional cooling effect. The symptoms of this exposure include general confusion, dizziness, nausea, redness of the skin, and not perspiring.

Finally, the human body is composed mostly of water. We can become dehydrated quickly or slowly, depending on the weather, trail difficulty, and our level of physical fitness, and we need to drink water accordingly. Carrying more water than you think you need is a critical safety measure. It is a good idea to also have a backup water filtration system such as tablets for sterilizing water or a portable water filter. People can go a long time without food, but they can't go a long time without water. Also, it is a good idea to start any hike already well hydrated. If your urine is dark in color or you haven't peed in several hours, you may be dehydrated.

Emergencies
Accidents do happen occasionally, so it's best to be prepared and know what to do ahead of time. When hiking in Korea,

always carry a charged cell phone. The emergency number in Korea is 119, and if you call, the service will supply an English speaker if you do not know Korean. Just be patient. On all national park trails and most provincial park and local trails, there are markers showing a numeric trail ID and an emergency number to call in addition to the national 119 number. This greatly aids park rangers and other first responders in locating and finding you quickly, so it's always good practice to make a mental note of these markers as you hike and remember (or better yet, take a quick picture with your smartphone) as you pass by.

Because a cell phone is the number one item to have in your pack in event of an emergency, keep your phone off unless you are actively using it. When going on a long or overnight hike, bring an external battery to recharge your phone on the go. You can also carry a cheap, disposable backup phone.

There are few places in Korea where a mobile signal is nonexistent. But it is possible that you could drop your phone and break it, or it could get waterlogged and stop working (it's always a great idea to wrap your phone in a plastic bag if there's any chance of rain). Do not solely rely on your phone for navigation or personal safety. Backups, like physical maps, are essential in case something happens to your phone while on the trail.

If you do need medical care, the Korean healthcare system is very user friendly. There will always be someone at hospitals and clinics who speaks English. You will usually be seen without much waiting, and the costs are much lower than what they'd be in the US, payable by cash or credit card.

Training

Smaller incidents can often be dealt with by applying some basic first aid and a short rest. It's a great idea to obtain basic first aid training from a reliable supplier and carry a small first aid kit on every hike. Just remember, it's always better to have one and not need it than need it and not have it!

First Aid Kit

A good first aid kit should include:

→ Tweezers
→ Antibacterial cream for cuts/abrasions
→ Pain killers (Paracetamol/Acetaminophen, Ibuprofen, etc.)
→ Emergency blanket
→ Electrolyte tablets
→ Water sterilization tablets
→ Antihistamine tablets (Benadryl, etc.)
→ Band-Aids (with a selection of different sizes)
→ Roll-type bandage
→ Sterile dressings
→ Small knife or scissors
→ Mini-manual
→ Whistle and lanyard
→ Hand sanitizer
→ **Optional:** Muscle and joint hot/cold cream and patches/sprays

The Buddy System

It's always safer to not hike alone. Not only can you steal your friend's extra dried fruit and granola bar, but more importantly, if something happens to you while on the trail, your friend can get help.

The "buddy system" means hikers rely upon each other and help each other out when necessary. This is especially important during longer and more arduous hikes, such as winter hikes, where knowledge of the trail and adequate gear and experience are paramount to ensure a safe, successful, and enjoyable hiking experience for all.

If you do hike alone, it's always a good idea to tell someone when and where you are going, and to let them know when you return home safely.

Hiking Gear

In every town, village, and city across Korea, regardless of size, you will find a mobile phone shop, a beauty salon, and a store carrying hiking gear. The larger towns will have whole streets full of hiking and outdoor shops, and many of the supermarket chains such as LotteMart and HomePlus will also sell hiking (and camping) gear. The larger Western brands such as Columbia and North Face are sold side by side with Korean brands NEPA, BlackYak, and K2. Korea will seem a bit pricey to Americans, but for those arriving from Europe or Australia, prices will seem normal.

In terms of quality, Korean goods are well made and robust. I have owned boots, jackets, packs, etc. made by Korean companies and have had good results with them. Oftentimes, the only hard part about shopping for gear in Korea is finding larger waist sizes (in excess of 110 cm or 42 in) or foot sizes (in excess of men's EUR 44 or US 11). If you fall into either of these categories, then it's best to bring hiking gear from home.

Day Hiking Gear

→ **Daypack** (preferably with a rain cover/water resistant).
→ **Small LED-type electric torch/flashlight.** This can be either handheld or a headlamp.
→ **Plastic bag** to collect your garbage.

→ **Suitable high-energy snacks** (nuts, dried fruit, dried meat, chocolate, etc.), preferably nonperishable.
→ **Suitable quantity of water** (minimum of 2–3 liters for the average-length hike). It's also a good idea to start your hike already well hydrated.
→ **First aid mini-manual and first aid essentials** (see First Aid section on page 30).
→ **Cash** (always useful if hiking or not!).
→ **Hiking boots or hiking shoes** (waterproof with good treads).
→ **Appropriate hiking clothing** (moisture-wicking and non-cotton). You should always carry multiple layers when hiking in fall, spring, or winter. An extra pair of socks is always a good idea in any weather.
→ **Mobile phone** (with battery fully charged!).
→ **Portable charger** for mobile phone.
→ **Toilet paper** (in a Ziplock bag) and a trowel.
→ **Lighter.**

Backpacking Gear (Overnights)

The core items from above, plus:

→ **Multiday pack** professionally fitted to your body (with a rain cover/water resistant). Do not overfill your pack (carry the weight appropriate for your size and fitness level).
→ **A sleeping bag** (with appropriate seasonal temperature rating).
→ **A lightweight bedroll** (a pillow is not necessary—just fold up your jacket and put it under your head).

➜ **Nonperishable snacks and freeze-dried meals.**

➜ Depending on what you plan to eat, **lightweight pots or pans**, **paper towels**, and a **mess kit.**

➜ **A small collapsible gas stove** (if you carry a stove, make sure to carry a lighter and spare fuel canister).

➜ **Suitable quantity of water.** (For multiday hikes, you won't be able to carry all your water on your back. For these hikes, make sure you have a gravity-fed water filter and are aware of locations of rivers and springs along the trail.)

➜ In addition to the headlamp/flashlight you always carry in your daypack, bring **extra batteries** and at least **one other source of light.** An ambient source, such as a lantern you can read by, is a great overnight option.

➜ **Baby wipes and/or all-natural soap.**

➜ **Spare comfortable (and dry) shoes/socks/ shirt.**

Optional:

➜ **A thermos with hot water** can be useful in making quick instant noodles or refreshing tea or coffee at the top of the mountain.

➜ **One or two hiking poles.** Hiking poles are a funny thing: some swear by them, while others don't use them at all. The fact is, they will save your legs (and your knees!) on a multiday hike, especially if you are carrying a heavy pack.

➜ **Crampons for your boots**, for winter/icy hiking. These are readily available, and very reasonably priced. Don't hike in the winter without them or you will pay the price with a slip and subsequent injury.

Hikes and Maps

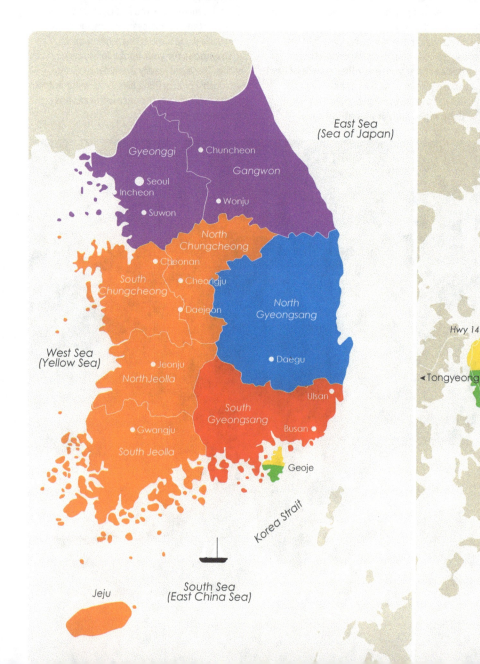

East Sea
(Sea of Japan)

Gyeonggi   • Chuncheon
                              Gangwon
     ● Seoul
Incheon
              • Suwon   • Wonju

                    North
                    Chungcheong
          • Cheonan
South   • Cheongju
Chungcheong
                    • Daejeon   North
                                       Gyeongsang

West Sea
(Yellow Sea)
                                   • Daegu
               • Jeonju
          NorthJeolla   ◄ Tongyeong
                              South
                              Gyeongsang   Ulsan
          • Gwangju   • Busan
          South Jeolla
                                    Geoje

                                   Korea Strait

Hwy 14

                    South Sea
Jeju   (East China Sea)

There are thousands of trails in mainland Korea and hundreds that crisscross Geoje. Many of these trails interconnect, allowing you to easily modify hikes to make them shorter or longer, or easier or harder. However, I have chosen those I personally know and can vouch for, such that I feel comfortable recommending them in this guide.

For mainland Korea, I have separated the hikes into four regions: North (including Seoul, Incheon, and the provinces of Gyeonggi and Gangwon); West (including Gwangju, Sejong, Daejeon, the island of Jeju, and the provinces of South Jeolla, North Jeolla, South Chungcheong, and North Chungcheon); East (including Daegu and the province of North Gyeongsang); and South (including Ulsan, Busan, and the province of South Gyeongsang).

For Geoje, I have separated the hikes into two regions: North and South, based on where they fall in relation to Highway 14, which bisects the island roughly in the middle.

In the hike descriptions, you will come across the terms "point to point" (or one way), "out and back" (also known as a "route"), and "loop." When hiking point to point, note that transportation must be arranged to pick you up at the finish and return you to the start—or to your hotel/home. In the hike details, you will find out what type of hike it is (point to point, out and back, or loop) and what options may be available to make a route a loop.

For the distance, the number I have provided refers to the total distance—whether out and back, loop, or one-way route. In other words, the distance for all out and back hikes includes the return. Time on the trail is also for the entire hike, including stops, unless otherwise specified. I provide both distances and elevations using the metric system (meters and kilometers), as that is the measurement system used in Korea. This may be an adjustment for hikers from the US, but I promise you'll get used to it in no time. When in doubt, there are several helpful apps and websites that can quickly do the conversion to feet and miles for you.

Legend

Road	
Route (one direction)	
Route (both directions)	
Alternative Route	
Cable Car	
Direction	
Start / Finish	
Point of Interest	
Bridge	
Stairs	

Parking	
Toilets/WC	
Gazebo	
Gate	
Temple	
Restaurant	
Summit	
Lookout Point	
Tunnel	

Note that the Korean words "san" or "bong" indicate a mountain or a peak. In addition, I have occasionally also used "Mt." for mountain. This dual usage covers all the bases for increased clarity, even if it's not 100 percent correct and may duplicate meanings in the two languages. For temples, I have typically stuck to the Korean usage of "sa" after the temple's name (e.g., Tongdosa). When the temple is very small, or the name of the temple is unknown, I have simply marked it as "temple" on the maps.

Note also that several hikes reference landmarks such as coffee shops, convenience stores, apartment complexes, schools, grocery stores, hotels, and other businesses. These locations were all current at the writing of this book, but they may have changed form or disappeared completely since then. I have made every effort to ensure that no hike description is solely dependent on these potentially transient landmarks. When in doubt, consult the GPS coordinates that I have provided.

The maps in this guidebook originally drew from open-source maps at d-maps.com and from my own experience, having personally hiked all of the trails. A professional mapmaker then took these renderings and notes and carefully crafted the beautiful maps you will find in this guide. Please refer to the legend for the meaning of common symbols you will find on the maps.

You will see the words "gazebo," "hut," and "shelter" on the maps. Typically, a gazebo is an open-air shelter with a roof and floor, oftentimes elevated, with benches around the inside circumference, similar to what you might commonly see in a park or botanical garden. A hut, or mountain hut, is typically a place where some type of meal or refreshments may be available. I use the term shelter as an all-encompassing word for a covered area of some kind; it will have an area for rest and may also offer food. Typically, none of these places offer overnight accommodations or camping, though they will be happy to provide temporary shelter from the elements for anyone needing it.

It's important to note that all but one of the hikes featured in this hiking guide are intended to be day hikes (albeit a few very long and strenuous ones!), so I have generally not included any information about overnight stays or camping along the trail. Typically, free "wild" camping is not allowed in Korean national parks outside of designated campgrounds.

As a supplement to this guide, especially for hiking in Korean national parks, another outstanding resource is the government website https://english.knps.or.kr. The equivalent of Google Maps in Korea is Naver Maps, found at https://map.naver.com. The latter maps are in Korean, but they can be used by anyone. You will be able to see many trails (in green) and important details, such as the location of potable water, temples, stairs, distances, estimated time ascending/descending, and bus/metro stops at trailheads/junctions. It's worthwhile to invest a little time becoming familiar with Naver Maps, and don't let the Korean Hangul writing scare you!

Note: The KNPS frequently closes trails for remediation work and during high-risk seasons for forest fires and avalanche. When a trail is closed, it will show on the Naver Map as red instead of green. If you are planning on using a trail in the late autumn through early spring, it's always best to call the National Park Ranger before visiting to make sure the trail conditions are conducive to safe hiking.

Rating System for Hikes

It's a fact of life that some people are more fit than others. A hill climbed by one person in an hour may take another 2 hours or more. As a rough rule of thumb, and from many years of observation, typical speeds on the trail for the "average" foreign hiker vary from 10–20 minutes/kilometer on easy trails to 60 minutes/kilometer on challenging terrain.

Please consider that a hike is not race, and there is no reason to rush through it. If you find yourself rushing to get to a summit, break a personal record, or beat your friends, I recommend slowing down and enjoying the process. For Type-A people, sometimes this takes practice. When hiking in a group, differing abilities should be taken into consideration so no one has to feel pushed or let down by the pace of the group. I walk a bit slow because I'm used to hiking with children. A slower pace allows me to take more pictures and enjoy nature and my kids, so I'm happy.

The rating system for the hikes in this guide is based on my own experience and factors in trail length, total elevation gain, and discontinuity (that up-down-up-down ridge vs. a nice, steady slope). It's important to keep in mind that real-time trail conditions (icy, muddy, overgrown, etc.), and weather conditions (humid, snowy, rainy, windy, etc.) could change

any of the hike's ratings, so take due care, always.

Please remember that it is always an option to take a rest or even turn around and go back. Never feel pressured to reach a summit or keep up with your hiking companions. It is up to you to know your own body and your limits. Accidents usually happen when people are pushing themselves, and it's dangerous to ignore the messages when your body is telling you that you're done for the day.

Easy

These family-friendly hikes will have little total elevation gain (typically less than 50–150 meters). The easy hikes on Geoje have round-trip distances from approx-

imately 500 meters up to 8 kilometers, longer off island. They typically have covered gazebo-style rest areas and/or WC facilities, and may even be stroller friendly (for some or all of the distance), although in my experience a well-made and correctly fitting backpack-style carrier is a better option for you and baby both. If the hike is accessible for a stroller, I have indicated it clearly in the hike details. Easy hikes will have many options for taking a side trail to lengthen the hike as well as ways to comfortably shorten the hike. You could wear a pair of sneakers on these hikes, although I always recommend hiking boots.

Moderate

Total elevation gain increases to approx-imately 500–900 meters, and there are many more steep slopes, switchbacks, loose rocks, and discontinuous elevation along the trail. The moderate hikes on Geoje have round-trip distances of approximately 6–10 kilometers, longer for off island. There will be shelters but fewer of them (there will almost always be one at or near the summit). A moderate hike will require hiking boots. Definitely **do not** wear sneakers on these hikes.

Difficult

Total elevation gain on difficult hikes will be anywhere from 700–2,000

meters and may include all manner of steep rocky slopes and vertigo-inducing exposed ledges. The difficult hikes on Geoje have round-trip distances from approximately 10–20 kilometers, longer for off island. These hikes will have their challenges—such as scraping along scree slopes and leaping across streams, among other obstacles. Expect ropes/chains/steel ladders hammered or drilled into rock faces to assist in the traverse.

There may or may not be shelters on difficult hikes. In the largest and most popular national parks (e.g., Jirisan and Soraksan), you may find lodges on the higher mountain ridges with rustic bunkhouses that can be booked for the night. Please make such bookings in advance, as there may not be room. Such shelters will also typically have food and drink available, typically consisting of pre-cooked rice, instant noodles, and water (either from a spring or from bottles, or both). They may also have canned coffee as well (usually served cold).

A difficult hike will definitely require hiking boots. You want boots with a tough Vibram-style sole, and they must be waterproof, with good support provided to the ankle.

Very Difficult

Very difficult hikes include the same features of difficult hikes, with even longer distance involved or extremes in topography, or both. Only one hike in this book is intended as a multiday trip, requiring an overnight stay in a tent or lodge. The rest are very long day hikes, requiring enough stamina for 12–16 hours on the trail in a single day, with elevation gains in excess of 2,000 meters per day and distances in excess of 28 kilometers. Many hikes in this category require an early start or a late finish, making a good headlamp a must. One thing is assured: you will never forget these hikes (even if you want to)!

Master Hiking Index

N

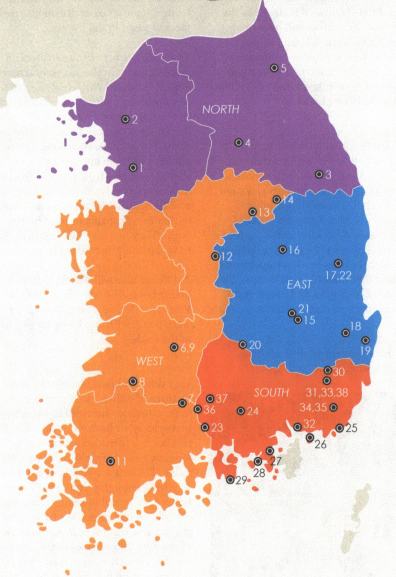

Mainland South Korea

HIKE #	HIKE NAME	DIFFICULTY RATING	DISTANCE	ELEVATION GAIN	STROLLER FRIENDLY	TYPE	LOCATION
1	Hwaseong Fortress Loop	MODERATE	8 km	125 m	No	Loop	Northern South Korea
2	Bukhansan Summit Loop	MODERATE	13 km	800 m	No	Loop	Northern South Korea
3	Ridgeline Route to the Coal Museum	MODERATE	13.6 km	600 m	No	Point to Point	Northern South Korea
4	Birobong Summit and Ridgeline Route	DIFFICULT	25.5 km	1,600 m	No	Point to Point	Northern South Korea
5	Dragon's Back Trail to Summit	VERY DIFFICULT	27 km	2,500 m	No	Loop	Northern South Korea
6	Valley and Tapsa Route	EASY	5.2 km	250 m	See hike notes	Out and Back	Western South Korea
7	Seongsamjae Pass to Nogodan Peak Route	EASY	5.5 km	400 m	No	Out and Back	Western South Korea
8	Eight Summits Loop	MODERATE	15 km	990 m	No	Loop	Western South Korea
9	Tapsa Ridgeline Loop via the Golden Temple	MODERATE	8.2 km	550 m	No	Loop	Western South Korea
10	Hallasan Summit Route	MODERATE	19.6 km	1,500 m	No	Point to Point	Western South Korea
11	Skybridge Route to Dogapsa	DIFFICULT	10 km	1,250 m	No	Point to Point	Western South Korea
12	Ridgeline Loop via Beopjusa	DIFFICULT	18 km	1,000 m	No	Loop	Western South Korea
13	Yeongbong Summit Route	DIFFICULT	12 km	1,800 m	No	Point to Point	Western South Korea
14	Birobong Summit and Observatory Route	DIFFICULT	19 km	1,100 m	No	Point to Point	Western South Korea

HIKE #	HIKE NAME	DIFFICULTY RATING	DISTANCE	ELEVATION GAIN	STROLLER FRIENDLY	TYPE	LOCATION
15	Gatbawi Buddha Route	EASY	3.8 km	450 m	No	Out and Back	Eastern South Korea
16	Hahoe Folk Village and Riverwalk Loop	EASY	3 km	10 m	Yes	Loop	Eastern South Korea
17	Valley and Twin Waterfall Route	EASY	11 km	120 m	See hike notes	Out and Back	Eastern South Korea
18	Gyeongju Ancient History Loop	EASY	9.5 km	10 m	Yes	Loop	Eastern South Korea
19	Seokguram Grotto to Bulguksa Route	EASY	4.8 km	400 m	No	Point to Point	Eastern South Korea
20	Twin Summits and Haeinsa Route	MODERATE	10.8 km	1,170 m	No	Point to Point	Eastern South Korea
21	Palgonsan Summit to Gatbawi Route	MODERATE	16 km	2,400 m	No	Point to Point	Eastern South Korea
22	Mountain and Waterfall Double-Back Loop	MODERATE	16 km	950 m	No	Loop	Eastern South Korea
23	Hadong History Park and River Overlook Route	EASY	2.5 km	100 m	No	Out and Back	Southern South Korea
24	Jinjuseong Riverwalk and Museum Loop	EASY	3 km	50 m	Yes	Loop	Southern South Korea
25	Igidae Park Costal Trail Route	EASY	4.7 km	100 m	No	Point to Point	Southern South Korea
26	Yeondaebong Summit Loop	EASY	4.8 km	300 m	No	Loop	Southern South Korea
27	Cable Car to Mireuksan Summit	EASY	0.6 km	80 m	No	Out and Back	Southern South Korea
28	Saryang Island Ridgeline Route	EASY	7.5 km	400 m	No	Point to Point	Southern South Korea
29	Boriamsa Route	EASY	2.5 km	150 m	See hike notes	Out and Back	Southern South Korea
30	Seongnamsa Route	MODERATE	10.5 km	650 m	No	Point to Point	Southern South Korea

HIKE #	HIKE NAME	DIFFICULTY RATING	DISTANCE	ELEVATION GAIN	STROLLER FRIENDLY	TYPE	LOCATION
31	Eastern Route to Valley Floor	MODERATE	16.5 km	800 m	No	Point to Point	Southern South Korea
32	Jinhae Ridge Circuit Route	MODERATE	24 km	700 m	No	Point to Point	Southern South Korea
33	Western Route to Pyochungsa	MODERATE	11.5 km	700 m	No	Point to Point	Southern South Korea
34	Beomeosa, Geumseong Fortress, and Godangbong Summit Route	MODERATE	6 km	550 m	No	Out and Back	Southern South Korea
35	Beomeosa, Geumseong Fortress, and Botanical Gardens Route	MODERATE	12.5 km	550 m	No	Point to Point	Southern South Korea
36	Twin Peaks Southwestern Route	DIFFICULT	26 km	1,600 m	No	Point to Point	Southern South Korea
37	Cheonwangbong Summit Southeastern Loop	DIFFICULT	19 km	1,450 m	No	Loop	Southern South Korea
38	Eastern Route to Tongdosa	DIFFICULT	23 km	900 m	No	Point to Point	Southern South Korea

Geoje Island

39	Gohyeon Fortress Loop	EASY	850 m	20 m	Yes	Loop	North Geoje
40	Gohyeon Riverwalk Loop	EASY	2 km	10 m	Yes	Loop	North Geoje
41	POW Camp Loop	EASY	900 m	25 m	See hike notes	Loop	North Geoje
42	Gohyeon/Suwol Two Valley Overlook Loop	EASY	3.5 km	300 m	No	Loop	North Geoje
43	Suwol Stone Statue Loop	EASY	4.6 km	250 m	No	Loop	North Geoje
44	Rice Paddy Three-Way Bridge Loop	EASY	2.5 km	3 m	Yes	Loop	North Geoje

HIKE #	HIKE NAME	DIFFICULTY RATING	DISTANCE	ELEVATION GAIN	STROLLER FRIENDLY	TYPE	LOCATION
45	Chilcheon Island Footbridge Overlook Loop	EASY	1.8 km	75 m	See hike notes	Loop	North Geoje
46	Picnic Point Lookout	EASY	500 m	30 m	No	Out and Back	North Geoje
47	Daegeumsan Summit Loop	EASY	3.6 km	320 m	No	Loop	North Geoje
48	Pacific Codfish Trail	EASY	2.2 km	225 m	No	Out and Back	North Geoje
49	Deokpo Beach to Gangnamsan Smoke Tower Route	EASY	2.4 km	200 m	No	Out and Back	North Geoje
50	Deokpo Beach to Okpo Great Victory Park Downhill Loop	EASY	2.5 km	150 m	See hike notes	Loop	North Geoje
51	Okpo International Park	EASY	0.7 km	25 m	See hike notes	Loop	North Geoje
52	Okpo to Deokpo Beach Loop via Okpo Great Victory Park	EASY	6 km	150 m	No	Loop	North Geoje
53	Battleship Park and Okpo Waterfront	EASY	1.5 km	none	Yes	Loop	North Geoje
54	Yangjam Lighthouse via Neungpo-dong Sculpture Park Loop	EASY	5 km	150 m	See hike notes	Loop	North Geoje
55	Camelia (Jisimdo) Island Loop Route	EASY	3.8 km	50 m	See hike notes	Loop	North Geoje
56	Gyeryongsan Summit and Ridgeline Loop	MODERATE	6.6 km	500 m	No	Loop	North Geoje
57	Gyeryongsan Summit via Geoje City Hall Loop	MODERATE	5.2 km	500 m	No	Loop	North Geoje
58	Aengsan Summit Route	MODERATE	5 km	450 m	No	Out and Back	North Geoje

HIKE #	HIKE NAME	DIFFICULTY RATING	DISTANCE	ELEVATION GAIN	STROLLER FRIENDLY	TYPE	LOCATION
59	Daegeumsan Summit Route	MODERATE	4 km	320 m	No	Out and Back	North Geoje
60	Guksabong (and Little Giksabong) Summit Route	MODERATE	5.2 km	475 m	No	Out and Back	North Geoje
61	Guksabong Summit Loop Route via ISK School	MODERATE	4.5 km	425 m	No	Loop	North Geoje
62	Guksabong Summit Loop via Aju-dong and DSME	MODERATE	7.2 km	425 m	No	Loop	North Geoje
63	The Okpo Admiral Hotel to Gohyeon SHI Hotel Route	MODERATE	11 km	425 m	No	Point to Point	North Geoje
64	Okpo to Daegeumsan Summit via the Forest Route	MODERATE	14 km	200 m	No	Out and Back	North Geoje
65	Okneyobong Summit Route	MODERATE	5.6 km	475 m	No	Out and Back	North Geoje
66	Aju-dong Stadium to Okneyobong Summit to Jangseungpo Harbor Route	MODERATE	7 km	475 m	No	Point to Point	North Geoje
67	Double Summit Traverse Loop	DIFFICULT	16 km	700 m	No	Loop	North Geoje
68	Okpo Circuit Loop	DIFFICULT	21 km	900 m	No	Loop	North Geoje
69	North-South Island Traverse	VERY DIFFICULT	58 km	3,700 m	No	Point to Point	North Geoje
70	Dundeokgiseong Fortress Ruins and Woodubong Summit Route	EASY	11 km	400 m	See hike notes	Out and Back	South Geoje
71	Botanical Gardens Loop	EASY	750 m	25 m	See hike notes	Loop	South Geoje
72	Mundong Falls Route	EASY	1.8 km	75 m	See hike notes	Out and Back	South Geoje

HIKE #	HIKE NAME	DIFFICULTY RATING	DISTANCE	ELEVATION GAIN	STROLLER FRIENDLY	TYPE	LOCATION
73	Windy Hill Loop	EASY	2 km	70 m	See hike notes	Loop	South Geoje
74	Fortress Ruins and Gun Point Overlook Loop via Gujora Beach	EASY	4.5 km	130 m	No	Loop	South Geoje
75	Wayheon Peninsula Smoke Tower and Dolphin Overlook Route	EASY	6.5 km	290 m	No	Out and Back	South Geoje
76	Gonggoji, Dolphin Overlook, and Pebble Beach Loop	EASY	5.5 km	150 m	No	Loop	South Geoje
77	Sanbangsan Summit Loop	MODERATE	7 km	450 m	No	Loop	South Geoje
78	Gohyeon/ Gyeryongsan Fire Road Route	MODERATE	17 km	250 m	See hike notes	Out and Back	South Geoje
79	Seonjasan Summit Loop	MODERATE	9.2 km	450 m	No	Loop	South Geoje
80	Bookbyeongsan Summit Loop	MODERATE	4.5 km	350 m	No	Loop	South Geoje
81	Bookbyeongsan Summit Traverse Route	MODERATE	2.9 km	350 m	No	Point to Point	South Geoje
82	Nojosan Summit Route	MODERATE	5 km	400 m	No	Loop	South Geoje
83	Garasan Summit Loop	MODERATE	8.5 km	530 m	No	Loop	South Geoje
84	Mangsan Summit Loop	MODERATE	8 km	390 m	No	Loop	South Geoje
85	Mundong Falls to Okneyobong Summit Loop	DIFFICULT	11.5 km	750 m	No	Loop	South Geoje
86	Jagged Ridge Route (Nojosan to Garasan)	DIFFICULT	9.6 km	800 m	No	Point to Point	South Geoje
87	Figure 8 Loop	DIFFICULT	16.5 km	1,050 m	No	Loop	South Geoje
88	Blood, Sweat, and Tears Route	VERY DIFFICULT	26 km	1,450 m	No	Point to Point	South Geoje

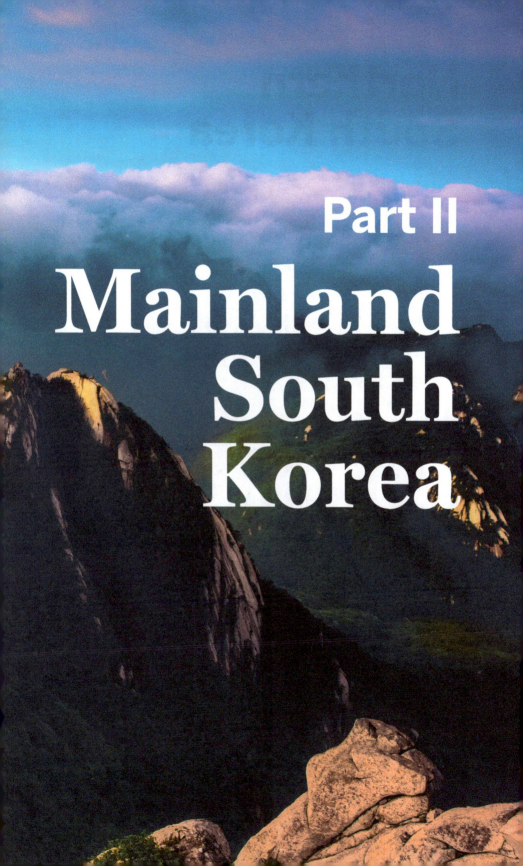

Part II

Mainland South Korea

Northern South Korea

N

North Korea (DPRK)

◎ 5

• Chuncheon

◎ 2

• Seoul

Incheon

◎ 4

• Wonju

1 ◎ • Suwon

◎ 3

Hike 1 MODERATE

Hwaseong Fortress Loop

🌐 **Location:** Suwon, Gyeonggi Province

⭐ **Rating:** Moderate

🔁 **Route Type:** Loop

📏 **Distance:** 8 km

🕐 **Duration:** 6–8 hr (includes a visit to the Fortress Museum)

⛰️ **Elevation Gain:** 125 m

🛒 **Stroller Friendly:** No

🚩 **GPS START:** 37.281888, 127.014511 (at Hwaseong Palace)

🔺 **GPS SUMMIT:** 37.280743, 127.010404 (at Seojangdae Command Post at 145 m)

🚩 **GPS FINISH:** 37.282476, 127.019004 (at the Fortress Museum)

 ## HIKE DESCRIPTION

This half-day hike and museum trip takes in magnificent city views from atop the ramparts of the fully restored walled city of Suwon, a UNESCO World Heritage Site. Suwon lies only 30 kilometers south of Seoul and is a large, modern metropolis. The city walls (including numerous gates, watchtowers, gun emplacements, and command posts) stretch 5.8 kilometers and are 4–6 meters in height. Each of the four main gates were fortresses in their own right, with additional defensive walls and various rooms built into them for garrisoned troops. Although the fortifications were built after the Japanese Imjin War in the 1590s (construction took place in the 1790s), it suffered significant damage during the Korean War in the 1950s. Fortunately, the damage was repaired in the 1970s.

For this hike, you will begin at Hwaseong Palace, where historical displays and martial arts are frequently reenacted for tourists. From the palace, follow the winding road and trail, which begins at the back of the parking lot on the south side of the palace grounds enclosure and climbs up the hill to the west. Halfway up the hill, you will encounter a road running north-south. Head in a southerly direction for about 100 meters until you reach the small, gated Sungshinsa Shrine, where a well-groomed path heads to your right back uphill, just passing along the south-facing wall of the shrine toward the ridgeline in a southwesterly direction. Once you make the ridgeline you will encounter the mighty stone wall with a pathway on the interior side.

Now turn to your right and head in a northerly direction. Soon you will pass the UNESCO World Heritage stone marker on your right, and shortly afterwards you'll arrive at the summit for today's hike at 145 meters. At the summit, there is the two-tiered Seojangdae Command Post with views in all directions, especially over the interior of the walled city. All of the main gates and the stream that bisects the enclosed fortifications are clearly visible from here. After enjoying the

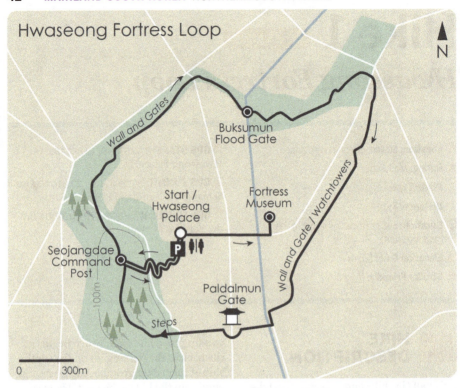

views, continue along the wall's interior trail in a northerly direction and descend toward the first of four main gates.

You will transition onto the wall itself for some portions of this hike. Note the impressive fortifications and the clever engineering allowing the stream at the Buksumun flood gate to be secured if necessary. Eventually you will reach the semicircular south gate of Paldalmun, which lies in the center of a busy roundabout. Once across the road, continue up the trail by following a series of steep steps until you reach the point where you first joined the wall earlier in the hike.

At this point, you have completed the wall portion of this hike. Next you will descend to the Hwaseong Palace following your earlier route. Walk along the grounds to the busy four-way intersection and cross the road heading in an easterly direction

for 300 meters until you reach the entrance to the modern Fortress Museum on your left. Outside of the museum are displays of large war engines, including trebuchets and similar siege equipment.

Once you've visited the museum, this day hike is complete.

Hike 2 MODERATE

Bukhansan Summit Loop

🌐 **Location:** Bukhansan National Park, Seoul

⭐ **Rating:** Moderate

🔄 **Route Type:** Loop

🥾 **Distance:** 13 km

🕐 **Duration:** 4–6 hr

🏔 **Elevation Gain:** 800 m

🛒 **Stroller Friendly:** No

🚩 **GPS START:** 37.656848, 126.946684 (at the parking lot)

🔺 **GPS SUMMIT:** 37.658707, 126.978093 (at Baegundae summit at 836 m)

📍 **GPS POINT:** 37.656408, 126.969198 (at Sangunsa Temple)

📍 **GPS POINT:** 37.657447, 126.964823 (at overlook)

📍 **GPS POINT:** 37.656275, 126.959297 (at Deogamsa Temple)

🚩 **GPS FINISH:** 37.656848, 126.946684

HIKE DESCRIPTION

Bukhansan National Park is located in the northern suburbs of the thriving capital of Seoul (population close to 10 million people), and is a convenient escape from the stresses, pressures, and crowds of the city. Bukhansan has many entrances and many, many, trails—all well marked and well worn due to the number of visitors.

For this hike, you will be heading to the highest point in the park, Baegundae, at 836 meters, on one of the most popular trails in the ROK. You will begin in a large parking area and proceed in a generally easterly direction, stopping at the KNPS Ranger Post to check the notice board for any trail closures (always a good idea wherever you hike). Grab a small pocket map here if available. Along the edges of the parking lot and the adjoining roadway entrance (which you will hike along for the first 2 kilometers) are many shops and restaurants.

Soon enough, you will encounter your first sense of solitude as the road meanders through the forest, rising slowly in elevation and passing through a large stone gate. Past Deoseomun Gate, continue on the trail, passing a small temple on your right-hand side. After 450 meters, you will cross a bridge. Following the trail markers, proceed toward the summit along the footpath, which is clearly marked.

The trail follows the course of a small rocky creek as the elevation slowly increases. For the first 1.8 kilometers, it is a relatively gradual incline, then it becomes much steeper for the next 650 meters to the ridgeline, where you will see a large stone wall and a gate. After passing the gate, turn left and follow the trail as it skirts along the wall and then climbs steeply. Note that several areas have chains, ropes, steel steps, and/or railings to help you ascend. The views become ever-more impressive, with downtown Seoul to the south and the

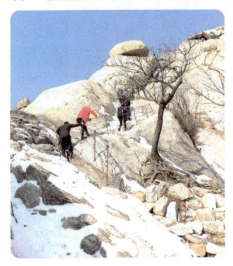

rocky granite peaks of the National Park surrounding you in all other directions.

Soon the summit of Baegundae, topped with the Korean flag, will come into view. Note that only a small number of hikers can access the peak area at a given time. Exercising care and patience, you must allow for "peak bagging jams" on busy days (which is most of the time). Once at the summit (surrounded by a steel railing to prevent any falls) you can enjoy unparalleled beauty in all directions while listening to the gentle flapping of the ROK flag high above you.

After enjoying the views, backtrack all the way to the temple turn-off point (approximately halfway down from the summit toward the bridge location) and then turn right, first passing a small temple and then a larger one (Sangunsa). At this point, you'll be heading back upslope to a second fortress wall and Bugmun Gate. Do not cross through the gate, staying instead on the southern side of the wall.

At the wall, turn left and proceed about 300 meters to the rocky overlook to take a rest and enjoy unobstructed views of the valley far below. Departing the overlook, follow the trail as it snakes along the stone wall, passing the hermitage temple of Wonhyoam. Keep an eye out for the trail down to your left with a marker for Deogamsa Temple. Once you find it, follow the trail as it descends the hillside steeply and takes you to Deogamsa, where there is a very tall Buddhist statue outside a shrine under a large rock slab.

After enjoying the Deogamsa Temple, continue on the trail heading in a generally southeasterly direction toward

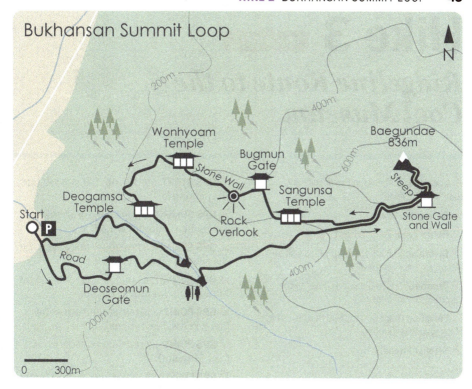

Bukhansan Summit Loop

N

200m

400m

600m

400m

200m

Wonhyoam
Temple

Bugmun
Gate

Baegundae
836m

Stone Wall

Steep

Sangunsa
Temple

Deogamsa
Temple

Stone Gate
and Wall

Start

P

Rock
Overlook

Road

Deoseomun
Gate

0   300m

the small river valley. After about 350 meters, you will come upon the river and cross another small bridge (note that this bridge is different from the earlier one), following the path immediately on your right, which hugs the bank of the river. Follow this trail back toward the parking lot (about 1.5 kilometers away) to complete this hike.

Hike 3 MODERATE

Ridgeline Route to the Coal Museum

🌐 **Location:** Taebaeksan Provincial Park, Gangwon Province

⭐ **Rating:** Moderate

〰️ **Route Type:** Point to Point

🦶 **Distance:** 13.6 km (14.6 km with a visit to Manggyeongsa Temple)

🕐 **Duration:** 7–9 hr (including a visit to the fairgrounds and museum)

⛰️ **Elevation Gain:** 600 m (800 m with visit to Manggyeongsa Temple)

🛒 **Stroller Friendly:** No

🚩 **GPS START:** 37.120408, 128.908453 (at the parking lot)

🔺 **GPS SUMMIT:** 37.098758, 128.915998 (at Janggunbon summit at 1,567 m)

🔺 **GPS SUMMIT:** 37.092099, 128.923210 (at Busoebong summit at 1,560 m)

🔺 **GPS SUMMIT:** 37.095046, 128.939956 (at Munsubong summit at 1,517 m)

📍 **GPS POINT:** 37.115918, 128.949188 (at Snow Festival Fairground)

📍 **GPS POINT:** 37.117166, 128.950206 (at Coal Museum)

🏁 **GPS FINISH:** 37.132156, 128.961253 (at the parking lot at intersection with Highway 31)

📖 HIKE DESCRIPTION

This hike can be enjoyed any time of the year but is especially rewarding (and beautiful) in the wintertime when you can catch the local Snow and Ice Festival, held in late January and/or early February since 1994. It is now the largest and most popular winter festival in South Korea. Adjacent to the fairgrounds there is also a modern museum next to the remains of a coal mine that brings to life this once-thriving industry.

You will begin the hike at a large parking lot and pass the entrance gate on the western end. From the entrance, turn to the south and follow the concrete road as it passes a few farms and enters the forest, climbing gradually toward the ridgeline.

After 800 meters, depart the road and take the clearly marked foot trail on your right and ascend toward the ridge another 800 meters.

At the ridgeline, merge onto the main trail and turn left, heading toward the summit of Janggunbon, approximately 2.2 kilometers away. As you approach the summit at 1,567 meters, you will see an ancient stone altar that was erected by shamans before the arrival of Buddhism in Korea. It is one of many altars (referred to as cheonjedan) atop this ridgeline. The site of ancient rituals, this area remains sacred ground for modern-day Koreans.

At the summit, there are expansive 360-degree views over the raw natural landscape with mountains in all directions. From here, you will continue on the ridgeline trail for another 500 meters until an even larger clearing is reached, with another ancient altar of hand-stacked stones. There is a clearly marked trail on your left, descending about 100 meters to the Buddhist temple of Manggyeongsa, about 500 meters away, perched on the slopes below the ridgeline. After a visit to this temple, backtrack uphill to the main ridgeline trail and continue toward Busoebong at 1,560 meters.

After reaching the second summit, you will now shift to an eastwardly direction as you head toward Munsubong, following the ridgeline trail through ancient groves of yew trees. The third summit at 1,517 meters features several large stone cairns amidst a rocky scree field. Enjoy expansive views to distant ridges and the surrounding forest. From here, continue in an eastwardly direction. After 150 meters, bear to the left at the trail junction as it descends through a forest. After about 1.5 kilometers, begin to follow a rocky stream bed all the way to the fairgrounds, which are about 1.6

kilometers away. The final stretch of trail merges onto a concrete road. Soon you will see the open fields of the fairgrounds, and in the festival season, the many snow sculptures, slides, food stalls, etc.

Following a visit to the fairgrounds, the Coal Museum lies only 200 meters to the northeast and is clearly identified by the large mine pit tower. The museum tracks the history of mining in the area with multiple exhibitions covering the geologic nature of coal, early mining methods, and more modern styles of mining, with full-size replicas and many pieces of mining equipment on display.

After the museum visit, follow the sidewalk in a northeasterly direction for 2.2 kilometers until you reach the junction with Highway 31. You can arrange a taxi from this location to take you back to the starting point.

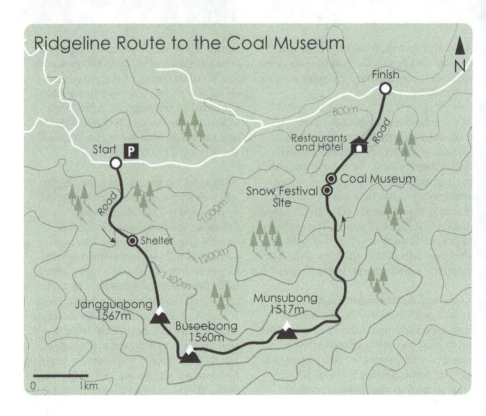

Ridgeline Route to the Coal Museum

Hike 4 DIFFICULT

Birobong Summit and Ridgeline Route

🌐 **Location:** Chiaksan National Park

⭐ **Rating:** Difficult

〰 **Route Type:** Point to Point

📍 **Distance:** 25.5 km

🕐 **Duration:** 11–12 hr

⛰ **Elevation Gain:** 1,600 m

🛍 **Stroller Friendly:** No

🚩 **GPS START:** 37.414740, 128.050413 (at the parking lot)

📍 **GPS POINT:** 37.399677, 128.049908 (at Guryongsa Temple)

🔺 **GPS SUMMIT:** 37.365084, 128.055507 (at Birobong summit at 1,288 m)

📍 **GPS POINT:** 37.306582, 128.053982 (at Sangwonsa Temple)

📍 **GPS POINT:** 37.305396, 128.030865 (at Yeongwonsa Temple)

🚩 **GPS FINISH:** 37.279737, 128.015190 (at the parking lot)

 ## HIKE DESCRIPTION

This long day hike is difficult not only for the terrain but for the sheer distance involved (nearly 26 kilometers). Adequate daylight is required, and hikers need to plan accordingly. Be sure to pack headlamps in case of an emergency. Note that there are no shelters or facilities along the entire route of the hike, with the exception of three temples, and all food and water must be carried. As with any hike, the weather forecast should be known before setting out.

Begin at the public parking lot about 1.4 kilometers north of the KNPS Ranger post at the northern entrance to Chiaksan National Park. Chiaksan, like its namesake "Sister Parks" Woraksan and Seoraksan, are all challenging in their own special ways. As a good

Korean friend once told me: "If you hear *ak-san* on the end, it means hard and rocky!" With this, you will now take on the rugged ridgeline trail in Chiaksan National Park.

Following the roadway and walking along the sidewalk, head in a southerly direction until you reach the ranger post, where the public roadway transitions to a temple road. Take the road for 900 meters up toward the magnificent temple complex of Guryongsa. After a visit, continue in a southerly direction following signs for the summit of Birobong, approximately 4.7 kilometers away (not to be confused with the identically named Birobong summit in Sobaeksan National Park, which is featured elsewhere in this book).

The road ends and the foot trail begins, traveling through a level forest and then climbing rapidly up a ridgeline.

Birobong Summit and Ridgeline Route

The views back down the valley and of the surrounding ridges become clearer and more impressive as breaks in the trees become more frequent. There is an observation deck about halfway to the summit. Finally you will emerge in a clearing atop the summit of Birobong at 1,288 meters, with two large stone cairns and a marker placed between them. From here, a keen eye can trace the remainder of the ridgeline as it heads to the south for nearly the entirety of the next 10.5 kilometers all the way to Sangwongsa Temple.

After enjoying the views, depart the summit and follow the well-marked trail in a slight westerly direction until you reach the main southbound ridgeline, proceeding all along the ridge heading south until you reach Sangwonsa Temple. Along the ridge, there are many openings in the trees and some rocky outcrops with views to the west over the city of Wonju.

After several hours of hard hiking along the long ridgeline, you will drop about 80 meters before Sangwonsa Temple comes into view.

At the temple of Sangwonsa, enjoy the views to the south from the bell pagoda, and after exploring the area, return back to the ridgeline trail and follow the signs toward the exit route. Be careful on this downward stretch of the trail, which is steep and wet and contains some areas of loose stones.

The foot trail ends at the temple of Yeongwonsa. From here, hike along the road for approximately 3 kilometers until the public parking lot appears on your left-hand side. Well done!

Hike 5 VERY DIFFICULT

Dragon's Back Trail to Summit

🌐 **Location:** Seoraksan National Park, Gangwon Province

⭐ **Rating:** Very Difficult

〰️ **Route Type:** Loop

📍 **Distance:** 27 km

🕐 **Duration:** 12–14 hr

⛰️ **Elevation Gain:** 2,500 m

🛒 **Stroller Friendly:** No

🚩 **GPS START:** 38.172869, 128.494601 (at the Seorakdong Visitor Parking Lot)

📍 **GPS POINT:** 38.174415, 128.486988 (at the Buddha statue)

📍 **GPS POINT:** 38.175998, 128.484823 (at Sinheungsa Temple)

📍 **GPS POINT:** 38.162609, 128.466434 (at the Biseondae Junction)

📍 **GPS POINT:** 38.132550, 128.464943 (at the Huiungak Shelter)

📍 **GPS POINT:** 38.121243, 128.460227 (at the Jungcheong Shelter)

🔺 **GPS SUMMIT:** 38.119184, 128.465387 (at Seoraksan/Daecheongbong summit at 1,708 m)

📍 **GPS POINT:** 38.140716, 128.467280 (at Yangpok Shelter)

🚩 **GPS FINISH:** 38.172869, 128.494601

HIKE DESCRIPTION

Gangwon Province lies in the ROK's far northeastern corner, bound by the East Sea on one side and the DMZ to the north. Gangwon is well known for its rugged beauty and offers an escape from the cramped confines of bustling Seoul, just 2 hours away.

This hike in the Seoraksan National Park (one of my favorite national parks in the ROK) is known among Korean hikers as the "Dragon's Back Trail." The name is inspired by the undulating and very challenging route used to ascend and traverse the mountain range toward the ultimate goal of reaching Seoraksan's summit at 1,708 meters. There are areas so steep and difficult that even using steel chains, ropes, and the occasional stairway,

you will still be lucky to make 500 meters of forward progress in an hour's time.

This is a very long hike, but fortunately there is a hut located at the approximate midway point (and an additional two more located close to the summit, plus one on the descent along the river/waterfall portion of the hike), but it's very important that you carry extra reserves of food and water. Additionally, due to the distances involved and difficulty of the route, it is likely that you may be starting in the dark with a headlamp on, and perhaps (read this as "probably") finishing in the dark as well. Expect the distance and topography to make this a long and challenging day on the trail! Unfortunately, there is no free "wild" overnight camping allowed in the park to make this a multiday hike; however, the Jungcheong shelter at the summit of Seoraksan (also known as

Daecheongbong) allows reservations, and any remaining spots are available on a first come, first served basis.

You will begin at the main KNPS Ranger post and Seorakdong Visitor Information area, which lies in the east of the park on the valley floor. Having paid the entrance fee, proceed in a westerly direction following the signs toward Sinheungsa Temple about 700 meters away. On your left, note the cable car carrying visitors to a high peak on the valley's southern side, which offers spectacular views across the valley and to the mountains in the distance. **(Note: From the cable car upper station, there is a fire road used by park authorities to access the summit of Seoraksan, but this is not a standard tourist route.)**

After hiking only 500 meters, you will come upon a giant Buddha statue cast in bronze on your right-hand side. From here, follow the trail as it bears to the left another 200 meters to the central courtyard of Sinheungsa Temple Complex. Following a visit to the temple, backtrack to the main trail and follow the signs toward the summit for about 3 kilometers until you reach a three-way junction named Biseondae. This is where the Dragon's Back Trail (#2 on the trail map) bears to the right. To the left is the waterfall route (#1 on the trail map), which will be your return trail.

From Biseondae, bear to the right and begin the long steady ascent up the stone steps and increasingly steep trail toward the first junction point (named Madeungnyeong) at the entrance to the Dragon's Back Trail. The distance from Biseondae to Madeungnyeong is 3.5 kilometers. Continuing on the trail, you now head toward Muneomigogae, which lies at the end of the most challenging section of the Dragon's Back ridgeline route, 4.5 kilometers away. On this section alone, expect up to 4 hours of hard hiking.

After reaching the Muneomigogae junction, follow the signs toward the Huiungak Shelter, which lies about 300 meters away—where you can collapse! At the shelter, water and food is available, thankfully. After rehydrating, cross the small grassy field and take the trail toward the summit of Seoraksan, ascending about 1.2 kilometers to Socheong junction and then bearing left toward Jungcheong junction, another 600 meters away. At this junction lies a comfortable mountain hut offering shelter and limited supplies for sale in season.

At this point (the Jungcheong junction, where potential overnight accommodations are located), the signs point to the summit of Seoraksan, which is only 600 meters away, and the final stretches of the trail seem to melt away one painful step at a time until you realize you have made the summit and are standing atop all of the northeastern Gangwon Province at 1,708 meters.

After a brief spell atop the summit, start to backtrack along the route to Muneomigogae junction, just 300 meters beyond the Huiungak Shelter. At this junction, you will now follow the signs toward the Yangpok Shelter (2 kilometers away) and Biseondae junction beyond that (an additional 3.5 kilometers past the Yangpok Shelter). This descending section of the route features a series of bridges that crisscross a raging mountain stream. There are many lovely spots along this trail to stop and enjoy the sounds of the stream and waterfalls.

Eventually you will reach the Biseondae three-way junction once again. Bear to the right and follow the rather flat trail back toward Sinheungsa Temple and the giant Buddha. When you finally reach the parking lot beyond the entrance gate you can celebrate having hiked one of the hardest routes in the ROK!

Dragon's Back Trail to Summit

Western South Korea

N

◎14

◎13

◎12

● Daejeon

◎6,9

◎8

◎7

● Gwangju

◎11

◎10

Hike 6 EASY

Valley and Tapsa Route

🌐 **Location:** Maisan Provincial Park, North Jeolla Province

⭐ **Rating:** Easy

🔁 **Route Type:** Out and Back

👣 **Distance:** 5.2 km

🕐 **Duration:** 3–4 hr

⛰ **Elevation Gain:** 250 m

🛒 **Stroller Friendly:** Yes (from the parking lot to Tapsa Temple only)

🚩 **GPS START:** 35.756761, 127.393425 (at the parking lot)

📍 **GPS POINT:** 35.758534, 127.411832 (at Tapsa Temple)

🔺 **GPS SUMMIT:** 35.761071, 127.410572 (at Maisan summit at 686 m)

🚩 **GPS FINISH:** 35.756761, 127.393425

HIKE DESCRIPTION

Rising out of the otherwise low-lying agricultural lands of Western South Korea is the jewel of Maisan Provincial Park with its two stone monoliths, known as the Horse Ear Mountains. Although the park is rather small and boxed in by highways, it offers unique topography (crumbling sedimentary-conglomerate rocks, not the typical igneous granite of most mountain ranges in Korea) and temples of many different designs, both traditional and unique. When visiting Maisan Provincial Park, be sure to also visit one of the many restaurants near the entrance, where you can sample wood-fired pork ribs with fresh rosemary, available by the part or full rack.

Start this half-day hike at the main parking lot and follow the paved roadway to the ticket booth and then past many shops selling a variety of souvenirs, including carvings, snacks, liqueurs with ginseng root, herbs, and snakes. Children will especially like the shop making fresh

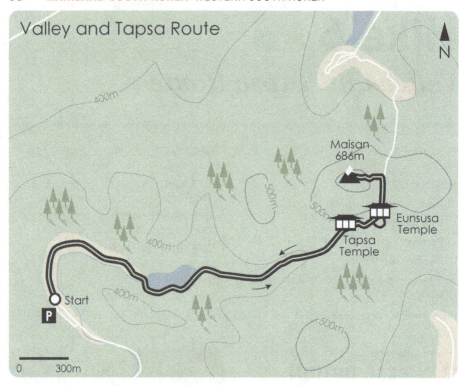

Valley and Tapsa Route

N

Maisan
686m

Eunsusa
Temple

Tapsa
Temple

Start

P

0　　　300m

rice cakes. A little farther along the road, on the northern side, there are many rustic restaurants with wood-fired ovens.

Begin to pick up your pace as you admire the beautiful valley and semi-karst mounds of stone all around. You will come across a temple on the left, and then a lake comes into view where row boats can be rented in season. Soon you will catch a view of the Horse Ear Mountains and arrive at the entrance of Tapsa Temple.

Tapsa Temple is a unique temple complex, not so much for its history (it's relatively new at only 135 years old), but for its construction and adornment, which consists of over 80 stacked-rock pagodas all assembled without the use of mortar over the course of nearly 30 years by one Buddhist hermit named Yi Gap Yong. Some of the tallest pagodas stand over three times the height of a man.

Once you have concluded your exploration of Tapsa, proceed up the well-marked stairs and follow the groomed trail to the small traditional temple of Eunsusa, only 500 meters from Tapsa. Passing Eunsusa, stay on the trail until you see the marker on your left leading to a steep ascent up to the top of Maisan. Once you have bagged the peak, backtrack all the way to the start point.

Hike 7 EASY

Seongsamjae Pass to Nogodan Peak Route

 Location: Jirisan National Park, South Jeolla Province

⭐ **Rating:** Easy

Route Type: Out and Back

Distance: 5.5 km

🕐 **Duration:** 3 hr

Elevation Gain: 400 m

Stroller Friendly: No

🚩 **GPS START:** 35.306542, 127.510929 (at Nogodan parking lot off Hwy 861)

🔺 **GPS SUMMIT:** 35.293793, 127.532172 (at Nogodan summit at 1,507 m)

🚩 **GPS FINISH:** 35.306542, 127.510929

📖 HIKE DESCRIPTION

This hike offers a high-altitude experience without the pain of a long and arduous climb. You will start at a typically well-appointed Korean roadside parking lot complex (named Seongsamjae), which offers several eateries, hiking gear shops, and a WC.

Begin the hike by following the broad fire road all the way to a hut. **(Note: Near the end of this leg, a 200-meter shortcut can save over 700 meters on the route. If you stay on the road, it will add an extra 1.4 kilometers total to this hike.)**

Passing the hut, the elevation increases in earnest. Proceed to the east toward the first large stone cairn marker (300 meters away) and then turn to your right and proceed up the protected trail with handrails. This trail heads about 600 meters to the top of Nogodan Peak, where a large stone cairn and stele

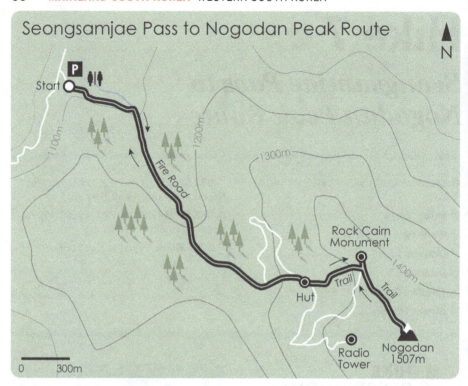

Seongsamjae Pass to Nogodan Peak Route

markers are placed. The views from the summit extend in all directions. To the west lies a radio tower about 500 meters away, but other than this one man-made structure nature reigns supreme. **(Note: The ridgeline, which runs 42 kilometers east to west, crosses the top of Jirisan National Park and can be hiked in 2 days, spending one night in a shelter hut atop the ridgeline.)** Once you have enjoyed the views, backtrack all the way to the parking lot to complete this hike.

Hike 8 MODERATE

Eight Summits Loop

🌏 **Location:** Naejangsan National Park, North Jeolla Province

⭐ **Rating:** Moderate

🔁 **Route Type:** Loop

📍 **Distance:** 15 km

🕐 **Duration:** 8 hr

⛰ **Elevation Gain:** 990 m

🛒 **Stroller Friendly:** No

🚩 **GPS START:** 35.487542, 126.907995 (at the parking lot)

📍 **GPS POINT:** 35.489566, 126.901834 (at Naejangsa Temple)

📍 **GPS POINT:** 35.493158, 126.905187 (at Baeglyeonamsa Temple)

🔺 **GPS SUMMIT:** 35.478429, 126.888948 (at Sinseonbong summit at 763 m)

📍 **GPS POINT:** 35.486510, 126.910260 (at lake with "Gazebo Island")

🚩 **GPS FINISH:** 35.487542, 126.907995

HIKE DESCRIPTION

This hike begins in a valley with two magnificent temples surrounded by high mountain peaks and will cover eight summits in Naejangsan National Park. The area is especially popular in autumn when the fall foliage is at its peak. If you prefer to have the place to yourself, choose a time outside the few weeks that the trees are ablaze with color.

Start the hike at the small parking lot abutted by a ranger post. Proceeding in a westerly direction, you will pass the gate following the paved roadway and walk about 500 meters along a gurgling stream to reach the heart of the Naejangsa Temple. After a visit to the temple, backtrack to the gate that straddles the roadway, then turn left in a northerly direction and follow the smaller concrete road (there is a marker and National Park map at this location) for about 700 meters as it winds up the slope

to reach the smaller hermitage temple of Baeglyeonamsa.

After a visit to the hermitage temple, which offers views along the valley and up toward the ridgeline, follow the trail along the easternmost wall of the temple grounds and start the climb up to the rocky ridgeline about 700 meters away. As the trail reaches the ridgeline, you will join a main trail running to the left and right. Turn left and proceed in a westerly direction to begin to hike the eight peaks of Naejangsan.

This ridgeline trail has many rocky outcrops and offers broad vistas both down into the valley and well beyond the park. There are no shelters on the ridgeline trail, so keep an eye on the weather (as always!) and come prepared with adequate water and snacks. Make sure to stay on the main loop from summit to summit; there are several branch trails heading downhill along this route.

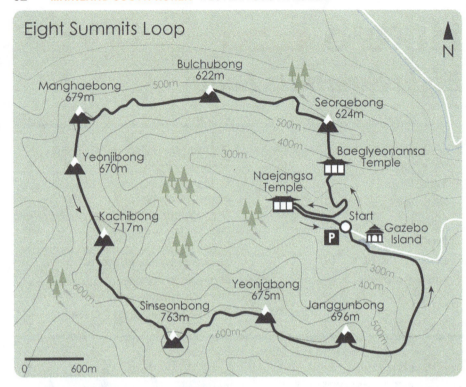

Eight Summits Loop

After many hours of hiking, with views looking down on the temples in the valley far below, you will reach the high point of the day's hike at summit six, Sinseonbong, at 763 meters. **(Note: The summit site is in a helipad clearing but is clearly marked with a stone summit marker.)**

Following the trail, you will make two more summits and then start the descent downhill toward the valley floor until you arrive at a trail that runs on the south side of the main roadway along the valley. Turning left in a westerly direction, you will soon come upon a small lake. On a small island in the middle of the lake, linked by a narrow causeway, there is a modern gazebo shelter. Following a short visit, continue on the trail for approximately 250 meters, passing many restaurants and stores, until you arrive back at the parking lot.

Hike 9 MODERATE

Tapsa Ridgeline Loop via the Golden Temple

 Location: Maisan Provincial Park, North Jeolla Province

⭐ **Rating:** Moderate

Route Type: Loop

Distance: 8.2 km

🕐 **Duration:** 4–6 hr

Elevation Gain: 550 m

Stroller Friendly: No

GPS START: 35.756761, 127.393425 (at the parking lot)

📍 **GPS POINT:** 35.760722, 127.389847 (at the Golden Temple)

📍 **GPS POINT:** 35.758534, 127.411832 (at Tapsa Temple)

🔺 **GPS SUMMIT:** 35.761071, 127.410572 (at Maisan summit at 686 m)

🚩 **GPS FINISH:** 35.756761, 127.393425

📖 HIKE DESCRIPTION

This hike begins at the same location as Hike 6 and follows the same return route after making the summit of Maisan. The difference is that before reaching Maisan, you will hike above the valley floor up to the Golden Temple and then onto a high ridgeline trail before descending back to the valley floor near the entrance of the famous Tapsa Temple.

Start the hike by passing the ticket booth and then taking the trail on your left, which starts flat for the first few hundred meters and then leads up several switchbacks and stairways as it climbs the hillside up to the ninth-century AD Geumdangsa Temple, also known as the "Golden Temple." This temple is situated atop a large bare rock, and it is quite striking because of its shiny golden appearance, which is unlike any other temple found in Korea. There is also a small cave below the temple with a shrine, and water is available

nearby from a spring if needed. The deck in front of the temple allows for fantastic views down the valley toward the Horse Ear Mountains.

Departing the temple, follow the trail through the pine forests as it rises and falls until you reach a gazebo shelter on a narrow rocky outcrop. Continue on the main ridgeline trail heading in an easterly direction. You'll pass two side trails on the right, which descend back into the valley.

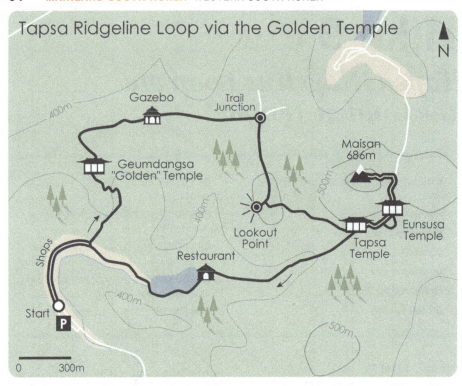

Tapsa Ridgeline Loop via the Golden Temple

N

Gazebo
Trail Junction
Maisan 686m
Geumdangsa "Golden" Temple
Shops
Lookout Point
Eunsusa Temple
Restaurant
Tapsa Temple
Start
P
400m
500m
400m
400m
500m
0   300m

When you finally reach a four-way junction (about 1.3 kilometers past the gazebo), turn right and take the trail, descending in a southerly direction toward the valley floor and Tapsa Temple. After one final stop at a rocky outcrop with views to the west down the valley and over the lake, the trail descends rapidly to the valley floor, and you will reach the main paved road just 100 meters from the Tapsa Temple entrance on your left. At this point, follow Hike 6 to make the summit of Maisan and return to the parking lot to complete this hike.

Hike 10 MODERATE

Hallasan Summit Route

🌐 **Location:** Hallasan National Park, Jeju Island

⭐ **Rating:** Moderate

🔀 **Route Type:** Point to Point

📏 **Distance:** 19.6 km

🕐 **Duration:** 8–9 hr

⛰️ **Elevation Gain:** 1,500 m

🍼 **Stroller Friendly:** No

🚩 **GPS START:** 33.422032, 126.549826 (at the Gwaneumsa Visitor Center parking lot)

🔺 **GPS SUMMIT:** 33.361311, 126.535735 (at Hallasan summit at 1,950 m)

🚩 **GPS FINISH:** 33.384953, 126.619727 (at the Seongpanak Visitor Center parking lot)

HIKE DESCRIPTION

Hallasan, the highest mountain in the ROK, is a dormant volcano at the center of Hallasan National Park on Korea's largest offshore island, Jeju. Despite the fact that its summit is the highest point in the ROK, the shallow slope of the volcano, coupled with well-marked, nearly straight trails, makes this otherwise long day hike a relatively moderate and enjoyable climb.

Although there are many trails in and around Hallasan (not all of which reach the summit), this route is a classical approach that starts on the northern side of the volcano at the Gwaneumsa Visitor Center and proceeds in a nearly straight line south, passing two shelters and a swing bridge en route to the summit. Note that along this trail, like all the other trails in this park, you will find shelters with WCs, snacks, and drinks. The eastern side of the cone rim is open to hikers, while

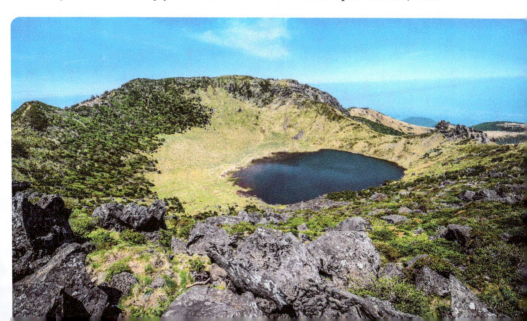

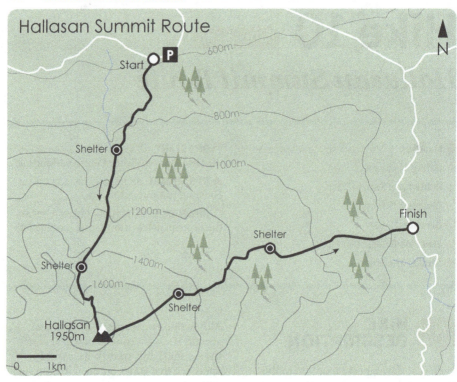

Hallasan Summit Route

Start

Shelter

Shelter

Shelter

Shelter

Finish

Hallasan
1950m

0   1km

the slightly higher western rim is closed to the public, so unfortunately, it's not possible to circle the cone. Many wooden platforms can be found at the summit location on the eastern side to allow the large numbers of hikers room to relax. Among these platforms, you will find a small summit marker for the obligatory summit pics.

After enjoying the summit, the eastbound Seongpanak trail leads hikers on the descending trail toward the Seongpanak Visitor Center parking lot. From here it is easy to take a bus or hail a taxi to make the trip back to the start point or any other location on Jeju Island.

Hike 11 DIFFICULT

Sky Bridge Route to Dogapsa

- **Location:** Wolchulsan National Park, South Jeolla Province
- **Rating:** Difficult
- **Route Type:** Point to Point
- **Distance:** 10 km
- **Duration:** 6–7 hr
- **Elevation Gain:** 1,250 m
- **Stroller Friendly:** No

- **GPS START:** 34.777413, 126.722509 (at the parking lot)
- **GPS POINT:** 34.771626, 126.716264 (at Cheonwangbong Temple)
- **GPS POINT:** 34.768875, 126.712341 (at "Sky Bridge")
- **GPS SUMMIT:** 34.766537, 126.703966 (at Cheonwangbong summit at 810 m)
- **GPS FINISH:** 34.753646, 126.659527 (at the Dogapsa Temple parking lot)

HIKE DESCRIPTION

Wolchulsan National Park is geologically unique in the otherwise low lands of the extreme southwestern corner of the Korean Peninsula. The mountainous area rises up from the rice paddies like an island of rocky monoliths packed into 57 square kilometers (Wolchulsan is the smallest park in the Korea National Park Service). This hike features a vertigo-inducing Sky Bridge about halfway up to the summit. You'll also find a temple on both ends of this hike. Despite the relatively short distance, and the modest summit height, the trail ascends and descends steeply throughout, creating greater total elevation gain and making for a challenging hike.

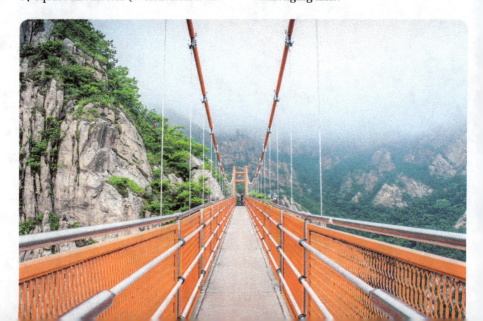

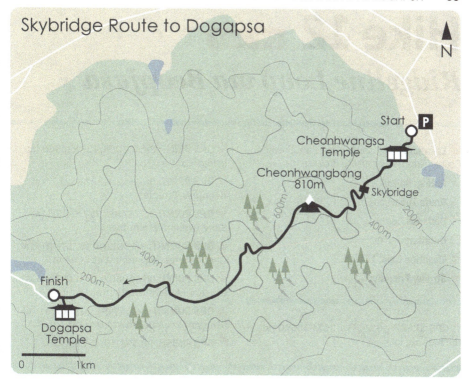

Skybridge Route to Dogapsa

Begin the hike in the large parking lot on the northeastern side of the park and proceed in a southwesterly direction, following the signs toward Cheonhwangsa Temple, about 900 meters away. Following a visit to the temple, continue on the trail as it quickly increases in elevation toward the Sky Bridge (aka the "Cloud Bridge"), a red steel suspension footbridge that is 52 meters long and spans a rocky chasm about 120 meters deep. Surrounded on three sides by towering mountains of rock, the bridge connects two stone pinnacles and offers views over the mountains and agricultural low lands to the southeast. Continue on the trail as it rapidly ascends and then drops off, giving up substantial gains before coiling upward again toward the summit of Cheonwangbong.

After following the numerous undulations of the trail, admire the far-reaching views over the rocky landscape from your vantage point of 810 meters at the summit. After a good rest, follow the signs toward Dogapsa Temple, approximately 6 kilometers away. At first, the trail descends from the summit and begins to flatten out, coaxing you into a false sense of ease before you again ascend and descend over the terrain. Eventually the trail falls off and becomes gentler as you pass through a forest until you suddenly break through trees and emerge into the courtyard of Dogapsa Temple Complex.

Dogapsa Temple has suffered much over the centuries (as has Korea herself more generally), having been burned down and destroyed multiple times from the Imjin War to the Korean War. It also suffered a fire more recently in the 1970s, requiring the Main Buddha Hall (called Daeung-bojeon) to be rebuilt in the 1980s.

Following your visit to the temple, proceed toward the main parking lot area to complete this short but impressive hike!

Hike 12 DIFFICULT

Ridgeline Loop via Beopjusa

🌐 **Location:** Songnisan National Park, Boeun County, North Chungcheong Province

⭐ **Rating:** Difficult

〰️ **Route Type:** Loop

🦶 **Distance:** 18 km

🕐 **Duration:** 7–8 hr

⛰️ **Elevation Gain:** 1,000 m

🛒 **Stroller Friendly:** No

🚩 **GPS START:** 36.533110, 127.823620 (at the parking lot)

📍 **GPS POINT:** 36.533068, 127.825860 (at bridge crossing)

📍 **GPS POINT:** 36.541914, 127.832957 (at Beopjusa Temple)

📍 **GPS POINT:** 36.547284, 127.859811 (at Sanghwanam Hermitage)

🔺 **GPS SUMMIT:** 36.543218, 127.870796 (at Cheonwangbong summit at 1,058 m)

📍 **GPS POINT:** 36.560302, 127.869463 (at the mountain hut restaurant)

🔺 **GPS SUMMIT:** 36.567997, 127.861744 (at Munjangdae summit at 1,033 m)

🏁 **GPS FINISH:** 36.533110, 127.823620

📖 HIKE DESCRIPTION

Songnisan National Park lies nearly in the center of the ROK. It has a huge temple complex (Beopjusa) within its grounds and many smaller hermitages. This section of the Bakdu-Daegan mountain range, which passes across the ROK from the northeast (Seoraksan National Park) to the southwest (Jirisan National Park), features exposed rocky outcrops eroded down by eons of rain, wind, and snow.

Begin this hike in the small tourist village public parking lot and make your way toward the hotel at the end of the road, headed in a northeasterly direction. You will then turn to your right and cross the small river (lined with cherry trees), soon arriving at a T-junction. There is a large National Park sign with an illustrated map of the park showing the main peaks of the Songnisan range, Beopjusa Temple,

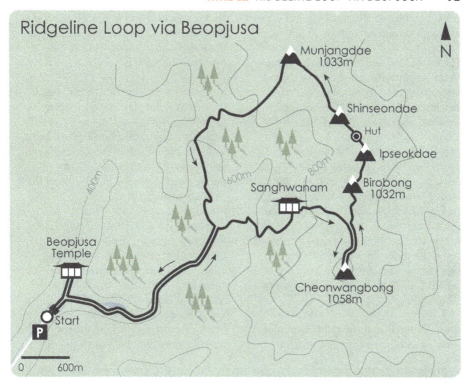

Ridgeline Loop via Beopjusa

and various trails up to the summit and ridgeline. Standing in front of this signboard, turn to your left and proceed to the ticket gate, where for a small fee you can gain entrance to the temple complex.

From the ticket gate, continue along the pathway for another 900 meters until you come upon a small bridge on your left-hand side. After crossing the stream, you will approach Beopjusa Temple, founded in AD 553 by the Silla-era monk, Uisin. Just outside the gate is an information board with a large map of the temple complex and more on the temple's history.

Pass through the main gate (past the temple guardians) and enter the central courtyard. The first items likely to catch your eye will include the 33-meter-high Golden Buddha statue, along with the five-story wooden Palsangjeon Pagoda

(Korean National Treasure No. 55). This is the only remaining wooden pagoda of its type in Korea, reconstructed in 1624 after having been burned by the Japanese during the Imjin War of the 1590s.

Once the visit is complete, depart the temple by crossing the small bridge and reaching the paved road. Now turn left and follow it in an east-southeasterly direction, passing a lake on your left-hand side, until you reach a small store and café with outdoor seating and a rustic wood charcoal-fired boiler to warm up by. From here, depart the roadway and follow the signs toward the hermitage of Sanghwanam and the mountain peaks of both Cheonwangbong and Birobong.

The trail crosses a raging stream and then begins to gain in elevation as the forest thins out just enough to allow for increasingly better views of the mountains above and the valley below. After about

1.2 kilometers on the trail, you will arrive at Sanghwanam hermitage.

Having visited Sanghwanam, backtrack to the main trail. Continuing to ascend, after another 1.4 kilometers, you will reach the ridgeline trail. To claim the first and highest summit of this hike at Cheonwangbong, turn to the right and proceed for another 600 meters to the summit marker. From the summit, which consists of a small stony nub surrounded by low bushes, enjoy the views over the rock-studded landscape. Having taken some time to rest, backtrack 600 meters to the junction point and carry on straight along the main ridge trail, following the signs toward Birobong and Munjangdae (about 3.4 kilometers from the junction point).

Approximately halfway to Munjangdae, you will come across a mountain hut

that serves cold and hot meals. A stop at this hut is very worthwhile, not only for the food (which is excellent), but for the far-reaching views!

Following your break at the hut, head toward Munjangdae along the rocky undulating trail. Soon enough, you will arrive at a large stone plaza with a huge, 2-meter-high summit marker and a tall steel stairway leading to the summit point, which is fenced in. The views from here are unobstructed.

Start your descent from the ridgeline following signs for the Buddhist hermitage of Jungsajam, about 1.5 kilometers down the trail. After a visit to Jungsajam hermitage, continue on the trail for another 3.3 kilometers until you arrive back at the small store/café. From this location, backtrack all the way to the parking lot to complete the hike.

Hike 13 `DIFFICULT`

Yeongbong Summit Route

🌏 **Location:** Woraksan National Park, North Chungcheong Province

⭐ **Rating:** Difficult

🔄 **Route Type:** Point to Point

📏 **Distance:** 12 km

🕐 **Duration:** 7–9 hr

⛰ **Elevation Gain:** 1,800 m

🚼 **Stroller Friendly:** No

🚩 **GPS START:** 36.915172, 128.100702 (near the bus stop on Hwy 36, adjacent to the Susangyo Bridge)

🔺 **GPS SUMMIT:** 36.886100, 128.106194 (at Yeongbong summit at 1,097 m)

📍 **GPS POINT:** 36.862205, 128.097466 (at Deokjusa Temple)

🚩 **GPS FINISH:** 36.863630, 128.087743 (at the Deokju Information Center)

HIKE DESCRIPTION

Woraksan National Park is well known for its rugged mountain peaks and challenging terrain. For this hike, you will begin on local road 36 at a bus stop adjacent to a small two-lane bridge that crosses the rocky stream bed to a small farming village. Having crossed the bridge (named Susangyo), follow the paved road as it bears to the right and then take the first left about 50 meters past a small store. Follow this road for about 2.2 kilometers as it steadily gains in elevation, passing by fields planted with an assortment of vegetables and a few apple orchards. As you near the end of the road, a small parking lot with a WC appears.

The KNPS trail marker and map is located at the edge of the parking lot and points the way toward the summit of Yeongbong, about 4 kilometers away. Just past the parking lot edge, the trail follows a road a little farther to a small temple (Bodeogam). From here, the road becomes a proper footpath, and you will continue to gain

elevation as you follow the trail markers through the forest, eventually reaching the first rocky spur with a large wooden observation deck. From this lookout point, the mountainous spine of Woraksan stretches out to the south while Chungido Lake and Reservoir (crossed by road and rail bridges) dominates the view to the north.

After a rest, push on through an even more extreme set of ascents and descents along the narrow and rocky mountain ridgeline, which includes mini-skybridges and many steel ladderways. The views along the route are exhilarating. About 1.1 kilometers from the summit, in the vicinity of Jungbong peak, a series of steep ladders hugging the near-vertical rocky route will provide both excitement and a little trepidation!

As you approach the summit, you will see the rock marker atop a narrow stone spur ringed with a handrail and accessed by a steep steel ladderway. If the trail is busy, expect to wait your turn to make the final 100 meters to the top of Yeongbong at 1,097 meters.

Once back from the congested summit area, follow the trail markers for the 5-kilometer hike to Deokjusa Temple, being careful not to take one of the side trails.

Continuing on the trail, descend the rocky ridgeline using a large steel staircase tower. Soon after reaching the bottom of the staircase, you'll hike a short section of protected trail under a loose cliff

into a rock outcrop, where you will be able to take a rest.

Departing the Buddha, you will now settle out onto more level ground and pass through a lovely forest that explodes with reds, yellows, and oranges in the fall. The broad trail now follows a small stream, and near the end of the trail, just before reaching Deokjusa Temple, you will cross a small wooden bridge over a waterfall before emerging out of the forest into a parking lot adjacent to the temple.

face. You'll then emerge back into the forest onto solid ground, passing along a ridgeline that falls off steeply on both sides of the trail. Soon you will come to a clearing that has a helipad. Cross the helipad area and stay on the trail, following the signs toward the edge of a tall staircase.

From atop the staircase, the trail becomes more difficult once again, and those with weak knees and ankles are about to feel the pain as the trail descends stairs and serpentine twists over rocky balds for a good 1 kilometer until you reach a small temple and a large stone Buddha carved

After a visit to Deokjusa Temple, continue down the paved road following the sidewalk for another 700 meters until you reach the Deokju Information Center, where a number of restaurants and stores can be found. Taxis can be booked from this location to ride back to the start point if required.

Note: There are many restaurants in the Deokju area that offer a delicious wild mushroom stew, with and without meat. If you have the time and appetite (I am sure you will after completing this hike), stop and enjoy this special local dish.

Hike 14 DIFFICULT

Birobong Summit and Observatory Route

🌎 **Location:** Sobaeksan National Park, North Chungcheong Province

⭐ **Rating:** Difficult

〰️ **Route Type:** Point to Point

🥾 **Distance:** 19 km

🕐 **Duration:** 8–9 hr

⛰️ **Elevation Gain:** 1,100 m

🛒 **Stroller Friendly:** No

🚩 **GPS START:** 36.933086, 128.554396 (at the Choam KNPS Ranger Post)

📍 **GPS POINT:** 36.944501, 128.525981 (at Choamsa Temple)

🔺 **GPS SUMMIT:** 36.973048, 128.506508 (at Gudmangbong summit at 1,420.5 m)

🔺 **GPS SUMMIT:** 36.957456, 128.484819 (at Birobong summit at 1,439 m)

🔺 **GPS SUMMIT:** 36.934167, 128.460726 (at Yeonhwabong summit at 1,383 m)

📍 **GPS POINT:** 36.934366, 128.456133 (at the Astronomical Observatory)

📍 **GPS POINT:** 36.919911, 128.457218 (at Huibangsa Temple)

🏁 **GPS FINISH:** 36.909021, 128.459415 (at the Huibang KNPS Ranger Post)

HIKE DESCRIPTION

Founded in 1987, Sobaeksan National Park is one of the newer national parks in the KNPS, and its open, well-maintained trails, good visibility, and extra equipment (handrails, rubber mats, etc.) allow for safer wintertime hiking. If you haven't tried wintertime hiking, now is your chance!

This area of Korea is less developed than many in the ROK and as such enjoys relatively dark night skies. The Sobaeksan Optical Astronomical Observatory (SOAO) lies just below the summit of Yeonhwabong at approximately 1,300 meters and enjoys clear views of the heavens above. During this hike, you will summit three mountains, see two temples,

explore a waterfall, and have a chance to see the observatory buildings up close.

Begin at the Choam KNPS Ranger Post and Visitor Information Center. Following the roadway (and signage), head in a generally northwesterly direction as the trail increases in elevation. After about 1.5 kilometers, you will reach the small Choamsa Temple. From here, continue on the trail, being careful to bear to the right at the trail junction toward Gudmangbong (do not go toward Birosa Temple).

The trail now rises steeply, and glimpses of the ridgeline far above start to come in and out of view. After hiking for 3.8 kilometers, you will reach the ridgeline trail. For the first high point of this great hike, turn to the right and hike

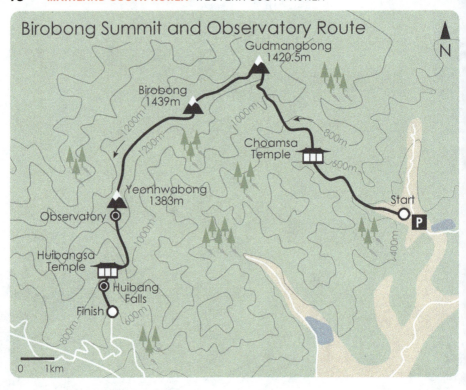

for 250 meters to claim the summit of Gudmangbong. After admiring the views, backtrack to continue on the trail, following signs toward the highest point of the day, Birobong summit. After about 2.7 kilometers, you will reach the top of Birobong at 1,439 meters (not to be confused with the identically named Birobong summit in Chiaksan National Park, which is featured elsewhere in this

book). Views on a clear day spread out across ripples of mountains and valleys as far as the eye can see.

From the summit, a clear and pronounced ridgeline trail runs to the southeast. In the distance, two towers are visible to the north of the trail. The first tower is lower, with metal dome-shaped roofs—this is the observatory. A little farther to the north is the second and taller tower—this is a government installation, which you will not be passing on this route, but it offers a good reference point throughout much of the hike.

Descending from Birobong using a protected set of stairs and walkway, you will encounter (after 400 meters) a small platform on the left-hand side of the trail that is shielded from the worst of the wind. This offers a better place to stop and enjoy a snack and (warm) beverage than the summit location. Following a

at the summit of Yeonhwabong, you now take the trail descending the ridge in a south-southeasterly direction toward Huibangsa Temple, about 2 kilometers from Yeonhwabong. This stretch of the trail is a bit more difficult.

Soon the small temple of Huibangsa will come into view. Just a few minutes below the temple lies an impressive waterfall (Huibang Falls) that is mostly frozen in wintertime. Expect a small rush of adrenaline as you cross a narrow steel bridge high above the gorge with views of the falls. From here, you can descend via steps to the lower pool at the base of the falls.

rest, stay on the trail and hike through a magical winter wonderland of low forests with ice and snow encrusted around every twig, branch, and blade of grass.

From Birobong, you will hike for about 4 kilometers until you reach the third peak of the day, Yeonhwabong. At this location, you can take the short side trip to the observatory or continue on the trail. Back

After the waterfall, stay on the trail for another 300 meters, and you will cross under a wooden arch and enter a small parking lot. Follow the road downhill for another 1.8 kilometers until you reach the final parking lot, which ends the hike.

Eastern South Korea

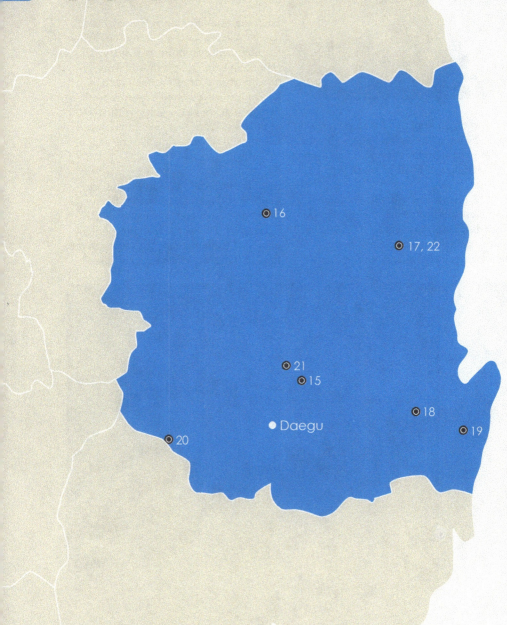

N

16

17, 22

21

15

18

Daegu

19

20

Hike 15 `EASY`

Gatbawi Buddha Route

- 🌐 **Location:** Daegu
- ⭐ **Rating:** Easy
- 〰️ **Route Type:** Out and Back
- 🦶 **Distance:** 3.8 km
- 🕐 **Duration:** 2 hr
- 🏔️ **Elevation Gain:** 450 m
- 🚼 **Stroller Friendly:** No

🚩 **GPS START:** 35.96999, 128.7265 (at the parking lot)

🔺 **GPS SUMMIT:** 35.97763, 128.7337 (at Gatbawi Buddha)

🚩 **GPS FINISH:** 35.96999, 128.7265

HIKE DESCRIPTION

The Gatbawi Buddha (or "Stone Hat" Buddha as it is sometimes called) is a designated National Treasure (No. 431) in Korea. Located at Mt. Palgong near Daegu, the Buddha was carved out of granite in AD 638 by the monk Uihyeon and is referred to as the wish-fulfilling "Medicine Buddha." You are likely to see many visitors here praying and making offerings.

The hike begins at a busy parking lot surrounded by restaurants. There are additional overflow parking lots available, as this is a very popular tourist and religious point of interest in Korea. Begin by walking up the road toward the mountain, gaining elevation with every step. After passing a smaller temple complex, the road ends and the stairs begin. There are many staircases ahead for this steep ascent, so prepare yourself. The trail goes straight up the slopes of the mountain to the ridgetop, where the Gatbawi Buddha is located at 850 meters.

To complete this hike, backtrack along the same route, passing the small temple of Gwanamsa at the bottom of the stairs, finishing at the parking lot.

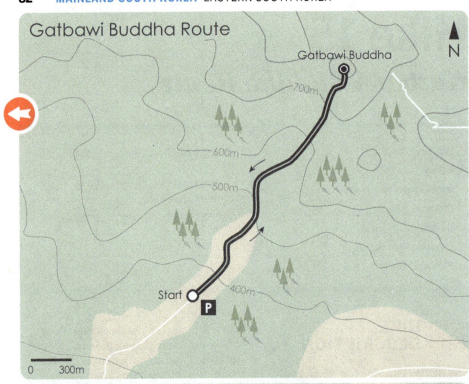

Gatbawi Buddha Route

Gatbawi Buddha

700m

600m

500m

400m

Start

P

N

0   300m

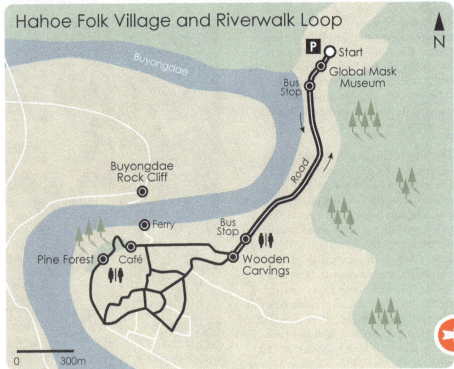

Hahoe Folk Village and Riverwalk Loop

Buyongdae

P

Start

Global Mask Museum

Bus Stop

Road

Buyongdae Rock Cliff

Ferry

Bus Stop

Pine Forest

Café

Wooden Carvings

N

0   300m

Hike 16 EASY

Hahoe Folk Village and Riverwalk Loop

Location: Andong, North Gyeongsang Province

Rating: Easy

Route Type: Loop

Distance: 3 km

Duration: 2–4 hr

Elevation Gain: 10 m

Stroller Friendly: Yes

GPS START: 36.550639, 128.529187 (at the parking lot)

GPS POINT: 36.541081, 128.516554 (at the benches in the pine forest)

GPS FINISH: 36.550639, 128.529187

HIKE DESCRIPTION

The Hahoe Folk Village is a major Korean cultural site located in Andong. The Ryu Clan has lived in this traditional village for 500 years, which was granted UNESCO World Heritage status in 2010.

Begin your hike by visiting the Global Mask Museum near the parking lot, which contains masks from all over the world. There is a sizable collection of Korean masks, including those used by the Ryu Clan in the Hahoe Village theatrical productions. From the museum exit, walk over to the ticket booth in a clearing southwest of the museum (about 125 meters away) and then proceed to the adjacent shuttle bus stop another 25 meters away. The buses are fitted with wide doors to allow people with disabilities and families with strollers to board easily. The bus will transport you to the main folk village entry area, about a 5-minute drive away. After departing the bus, you will see a large boulder carved with the UNESCO World Heritage details.

Continuing on, walk along the road toward the village, stopping after a short distance to admire a collection of wood carvings, some standing as tall as a person. Proceed toward the village proper and stop at the informational sign with a map of the village.

After a good exploration of the village, make your way to the river (Buyongdae) and visit the lovely old pines in the pine tree forest park (Mansongjeong). Located nearby is the local village café, from which it's a short walk back to the bus stop for the shuttle that will return you back to the main parking lot area adjacent to the Global Mask Museum.

Hike 17 EASY

Valley and Twin Waterfall Route

🌐 **Location:** Juwangsan National Park, North Gyeongsang Province

⭐ **Rating:** Easy

🔄 **Route Type:** Out and Back

👣 **Distance:** 11 km

🕐 **Duration:** 4–5 hr

⛰ **Elevation Gain:** 120 m

🛒 **Stroller Friendly:** Yes (however, there are a few sections with stairs)

🚩 **GPS START:** 36.390216, 129.141058 (at the parking lot)

📍 **GPS POINT:** 36.407483, 129.171129 (just past the Twin Waterfalls)

🚩 **GPS FINISH:** 36.390216, 129.141058

HIKE DESCRIPTION

Juwangsan National Park contains some minor but attractive peaks around a deep valley full of waterfalls and small hermitage temples. This hike will take you into the valley itself. Juwangsan is also located within one of the main apple-growing regions of Korea, so if you are visiting during the autumn apple harvest, expect to be able to buy a whole carton of freshly picked apples, which are extra sweet and crisp!

Begin at the large parking lot where a WC is located, then hike toward the park along a paved road that is lined with numerous shops and restaurants selling all sorts of hiking favorites and rustic foodstuffs. Notice the large bags of fresh ginger root (still covered in dirt) for sale

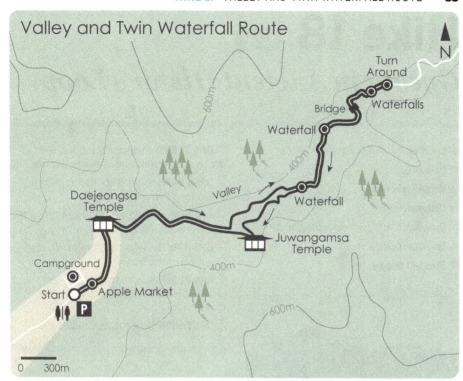

Valley and Twin Waterfall Route

and large vats of spiced makkoli rice wine with whole apples, ginger, ginseng, and other herbs floating in it.

After hiking about 1 kilometer, you will reach the ticket booth and entrance to Daejeongsa Temple. After exploring this scenic seventh-century AD temple complex, proceed on the trail, bearing to your left at the trail junction and following the main trail as it heads into the valley. A series of ramps, bridges, and stairs allows hikers to follow the course of the raging river below. Follow this trail, enjoying the many waterfalls until you pass over a bridge and then come across two waterfalls in succession about 450 meters past the bridge.

Just past the last waterfall, you will come across a trail heading up the hillside to your left. You will not take this trail. Instead, at the signboard, turn around and begin to backtrack to the parking lot. En route, take the short trail on your

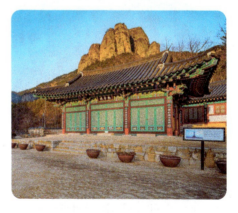

left to visit the small hermitage temple of Juwangamsa, which is reached by a rather steep series of stairs, set about 75 meters above the valley floor and surrounded by a backdrop of rocky crags. Afterwards, visit the nearby Juwanggul Cave shrine, which is located near a waterfall that becomes totally frozen in winter. After these stops, continue along the main trail back to the parking lot to complete this hike.

Hike 18 `EASY`

Gyeongju Ancient History Loop

- 🌐 **Location:** South Gyeongsang Province
- ⭐ **Rating:** Easy
- 〽 **Route Type:** Loop
- 🦶 **Distance:** 9.5 km
- 🕐 **Duration:** 6–8 hr (includes visiting exhibits)
- 🏔 **Elevation Gain:** 10 m
- 🛒 **Stroller Friendly:** Yes

🚩 **GPS START:** 35.830532, 129.228696 (at the Gyeongju National Museum parking lot)

📍 **GPS POINT:** 35.833420, 129.226808 (at DongGung Palace Entrance)

📍 **GPS POINT:** 35.833912, 129.224721 (at the film booth building)

📍 **GPS POINT:** 35.838343, 129.210462 (at Cheonmachong Tomb)

📍 **GPS POINT:** 35.834673, 129.219035 (at the Cheomseongdae Astronomical Observatory)

🏁 **GPS FINISH:** 35.830532, 129.228696

📖 HIKE DESCRIPTION

Gyeongju, once the capital of the Kingdom of Silla, which ruled about two-thirds of the Korean Peninsula at its height, contains an incredible wealth of ancient relics that date from the first to ninth centuries AD. For this hike, you will start at the Gyeongju National Museum, which brings to life the ancient capital's incredible history. Make your way from the museum parking lot to the large four-way intersection. Cross the main road and turn left, walking

along a series of reed ponds for about 600 meters until you see the entrance of DongGung Palace and Anapji Pond. Pass through the gate and make your way around the pond, enjoying the fine vistas and open-air exhibits under the pavilions. **(Note: There is a WC near the entrance gate on the inside to your left behind the building.)**

Exiting the gate, walk back out to the main road and follow it in a northwesterly direction for 150 meters until you find a crossing. Cross the road and stop at the small film booth building on your right-hand side, which offers a short film on the history of Gyeongju in its heyday when nearly one million people (representing 180,000 households) called this fertile valley home.

Continue on the path for about 350 meters as it skirts along the northern edge of the raised earthworks that once formed the Wolseong Fortress. Take the spur path that leads off to the left toward the Gyelim Forest. After 400 meters on this path, you will reach a short loop that passes small temple buildings and offers mesmerizing views toward the many burial mounds to the northwest of the forest.

After finishing the loop, proceed on the main path heading in a southwesterly direction until you reach the river and the covered Woljeonggyo Bridge—but do not cross the bridge. At the bridge, turn right and proceed along the riverbank, passing many cafes and restaurants until the next bridge, where you will turn right and head north along the main road. Just north of this bridge off the main road on your right is Hanok Village, a tourist attraction where you can enjoy period foods, dress in period costume, and find plenty of souvenirs.

Back on the trail, follow the main road north with the burial mounds on the right-hand side of the road in a large grassy field. Proceed until you reach a large intersection with a parking lot on your left and a foot trail to the observatory on your right. At this point, turn left and cross the road, walk across the parking lot, and enter the Royal Tombs Park via the gate. This park is a popular place for locals and visitors alike to enjoy fall foliage.

Follow the footpaths northwest until you reach a large tomb in the corner of the park named Cheonmachong. Excavated in 1973, over 11,000 artifacts were found within this fifth-century AD royal tomb, including some very impressive gold paintings and a crown. While the tomb itself contains a large exhibit, much more can be learned at the museum.

After enjoying the burial mound museum, return through the park back toward the entry gate. Once through the gate, proceed to the road junction and cross the main road, heading toward the observatory. After 400 meters, you will reach the Cheomseongdae Astronomical

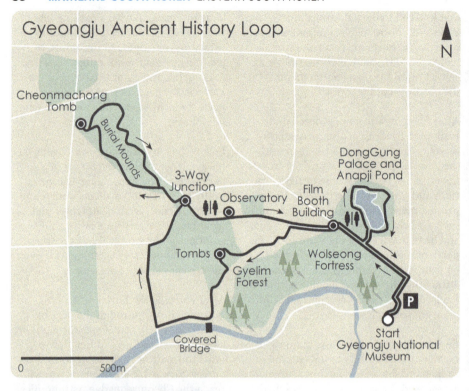

Gyeongju Ancient History Loop

N

Cheonmachong
Tomb

Burial Mounds

3-Way
Junction

Observatory

Film
Booth
Building

DongGung
Palace and
Anapji Pond

Tombs

Gyelim
Forest

Wolseong
Fortress

P

Covered
Bridge

Start
Gyeongju National
Museum

0   500m

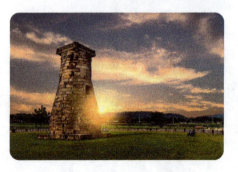

Observatory on your left-hand side. Built
between AD 632 and 647, the observatory is designated Korean National
Treasure No. 31 and is among the oldest
of its kind in Asia. Standing just over
9 meters in height, it represents the
sophistication evident during the height
of the Silla period.

After marveling at the observatory,
continue on the main footpath in an
easterly direction until you reach the film
booth building again. At this point, you
can proceed to the museum parking lot
or take a quick hike up the earthworks
on your right-hand side where there
are many trails available to the interior
of Wolseong Fortress. For nearly 900
years, this crescent-moon-shaped hill
fortress was the home of the Imperial
Palace, but today only ruins and a small
stone ice-storage facility remain. After
descending the earthworks, walk back to
the museum parking lot.

Hike 19 `EASY`

Seokguram Grotto to Bulguksa Route

🌏 **Location:** Gyeongju, North Gyeongsang Province

⭐ **Rating:** Easy

🔄 **Route Type:** Point to Point

📏 **Distance:** 4.8 km

🕐 **Duration:** 4–5 hr (including stops)

⛰ **Elevation Gain:** 400 m (all downhill)

🚼 **Stroller Friendly:** No

🚩 **GPS START:** 35.790662, 129.349798 (at the parking lot)

📍 **GPS POINT:** 35.791175, 129.349486 (at Bell Pavilion)

📍 **GPS POINT:** 35.794843, 129.349368 (at Seokguram Grotto)

📍 **GPS POINT:** 35.790022, 129.332175 (at Dabotap Pagoda)

🏁 **GPS FINISH:** 35.786084, 129.329735 (at the temple parking lot)

📖 HIKE DESCRIPTION

This hike visits not one but two UNESCO World Heritage Sites in Gyeongju. Start at the mountaintop parking lot for the Seokguram Grotto and proceed up the broad stairs to the Bell Pavilion, where, for a small donation, you can ring the large temple bell.

Continue to the north, passing the entry gate, and follow the serpentine fire

road as it proceeds through a peaceful pine forest on the eastern slopes of Thomasan, just 100 meters below the ridgeline. The fire road steps lead up to a small man-made cave, which houses the eighth-century AD Seokguram Grotto, with a stone Buddha that stands 3.5 meters tall. This marvel of Korean Buddhist art and architecture is both a Korean National Treasure (No. 24) and a UNESCO World Heritage Site.

Upon exiting the grotto, proceed down to the small temple to enjoy the views and clean mountain air before backtracking to the Bell Pavilion. At the pavilion, turn right and follow the well-marked trail, which leads toward Bulguksa Temple. **(Note: A trail nearby leads to the top of nearby Thomasan, elevation 745 meters, only 1.4 kilometers away.)**

The trail toward Bulguksa Temple descends all the way downhill, where you'll find a WC. As you near the bottom

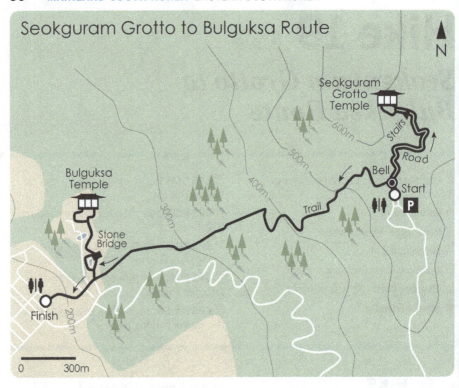

Seokguram Grotto to Bulguksa Route

N

Seokguram Grotto Temple

600m · Stairs

500m · Road

Bell · Start · P

400m · Trail

Bulguksa Temple

300m

Stone Bridge

200m

Finish

0   300m

of the slope, you will start to walk along a wall (on your right-hand side) adorned with clay tiles. Soon, temple outbuildings will appear through the trees, and you will emerge onto a parking lot. Turn right and proceed to the temple entry gate about 40 meters away. Passing through the gate, continue in a northerly direction for 100 meters until you reach a scenic stone bridge, which crosses a lovely carp pond.

After visiting the pond and enjoying the magnificent views back toward the mountain ridge, proceed back to the bridge and continue on the trail in a northerly direction toward the main Bulguksa Temple Hall and famous Dapotap Pagoda (which adorns the back side of the Korean 10 won coin).

The temple was founded in the sixth century AD, but the buildings have all been rebuilt several times, most notably following the Japanese Invasions (Imjin War) from 1592 to 1598, when the temple complex burned. There are many Korean National Treasures within the temple complex including the Dapotap Pagoda (No. 20). Understandably, the entire Temple Complex is now a protected UNESCO World Heritage Site, and hopefully it never again suffers harm.

Once your visit to Bulguksa Temple is complete, exit the Temple Complex and follow the pathways toward the large parking lot on the southwest side.

Note: Across from the parking lot lies a small tourist village with many restaurants and services for travelers. A taxi can also be hailed here to return you back to the top of the mountain ridge parking lot for Seokguram Grotto, where you began the hike.

Hike 20 `MODERATE`

Twin Summits and Haeinsa Route

🌐 **Location:** Gayasan National Park, North Gyeongsang Province

⭐ **Rating:** Moderate

🔁 **Route Type:** Point to Point

👣 **Distance:** 10.8 km

🕐 **Duration:** 5–6 hr

⛰ **Elevation Gain:** 1,170 m

🚼 **Stroller Friendly:** No

🚩 **GPS START:** 35.801277, 128.141933 (at the parking lot)

🔺 **GPS SUMMIT:** 35.822588, 128.122164 (at Chilbulsan summit at 1,433 m)

🔺 **GPS SUMMIT:** 35.823528, 128.120433 (at Sangwangsan summit at 1,430 m)

📍 **GPS POINT:** 35.800999, 128.097486 (at Haeinsa Temple)

🚩 **GPS FINISH:** 35.791714, 128.090024 (at the Gaya Village parking lot)

📖 HIKE DESCRIPTION

This is one of my favorite hikes in all Korea. Although it is a rather short hike, the natural setting and cultural richness of the ninth-century AD Haeinsa Temple make this a truly rewarding experience.

You will start this hike in a large parking lot, and after checking in on the trail conditions with the National Park Ranger at the entrance hut, proceed up the concrete road, passing small roadside stands selling a variety of wild mushroom teas, panfried potato-veggie pancakes, and similar hiking fare. After 200 meters, you will pass the Gaya Hotel on your right-hand side and the Botanical Gardens on your left. Keep following the road heading straight. About 150 meters past the Botanical Gardens, a parking lot will come into view.

At this point, you have to decide which trail you'd prefer. On the left side of the parking lot is the harder leg of the trail, which skirts a ridgeline over jagged rocks, dipping up and down along its rocky spine, until a three-way junction. Alternatively, you can go to the end of the parking lot and then turn right, crossing a bridge that passes over a small but raging mountain stream, and follow the easier route through the valley along a rocky stream bed up to the three-way junction. Either will take you to the same point.

Once you have made your way to the three-way junction, the unified trail begins. On the next section of trail, you will encounter several steep sections with ladders and platforms.

As you emerge onto a sharply inclined rock face with immersive views to the north and south, turn right and go the final 30 meters to make the summit of Chilbulsan at 1,433 meters, the first of two peaks today. This summit is rocky,

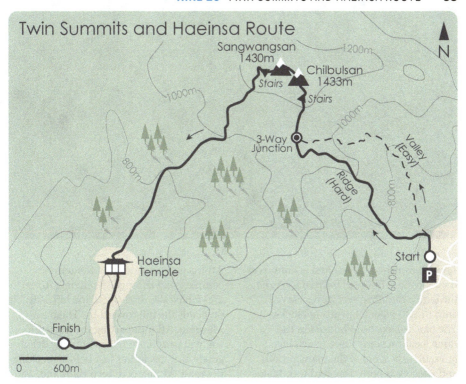

Twin Summits and Haeinsa Route

Sangwangsan
1430m
Chilbulsan
1433m
Stairs
Stairs
3-Way
Junction
Valley
(Easy)
Ridge
(Hard)
Start
P
Haeinsa
Temple
Finish

0   600m

and the area around the stone marker is small, so be careful here.

Return back to the main trail and hike about 300 meters until you reach the base of a large rocky outcrop with stairs at the base. Take the stairs up to the second summit of the day, Sangwangsan, which stands at 1,430 meters. A large round boulder marks the summit, and the

scramble to the high point just above and behind the boulder yields truly stunning 360-degree views.

Descend the stairs and take the trail that heads down toward Haeinsa Temple to your southwest. The trail descends over well-marked ground, fitted with mats in the marshy areas and bridges and stairs in the rocky areas. The final hour or so on the trail follows a rocky stream. Enjoy the sound of water cascading over small falls. As you approach the end of the trail, you will begin to see temple outbuildings and a small dam adjacent to the trail. Keep straight and soon you will pass a turnstile and a small ranger post at the exit of the trail proper. About 50 meters from the ranger post is a WC if needed.

Now follow the paved road up the stairs to the left to enter the Haeinsa Temple grounds. Haeinsa is one of the "Three

Jewel Temples" of Korea and is famous as the repository of the *Tripitaka Koreana*, the entire Buddhist scriptures carved onto 81,350 wooden printing blocks. The blocks have been housed in the same location since 1398, which has miraculously avoided the many pitfalls and ravages of both time and war. Make sure to take a glimpse through the open doors to see these cultural treasures neatly organized in row after row.

After a good look around the temple complex, exit through the main gate and follow the roadway to the left as it descends the hill toward the Haeinsa Museum. After departing the museum, you will pass more sellers of many dried goods and specialties just before reaching the road. At the road, turn right and proceed along the sidewalk for about 300 meters until you reach the parking lot and the tourist village. From here, a taxi can return you to the Gaya Hotel area.

Hike 21 MODERATE

Palgonsan Summit to Gatbawi Route

🌐 **Location:** Daegu

⭐ **Rating:** Moderate

📍 **Route Type:** Point to Point

📍 **Distance:** 16 km

🕐 **Duration:** 8–9 hr

🏔 **Elevation Gain:** 2,400 m

🛏 **Stroller Friendly:** No

🚩 **GPS START:** 35.992543, 128.702662 (at the Donghwasa Temple parking lot)

🔺 **GPS SUMMIT:** 36.015920, 128.692114 (at Palgonsan summit at 1,193 m)

📍 **GPS POINT:** 35.977630, 128.733700 (at Gatbawi summit at 853 m)

🚩 **GPS FINISH:** 35.969990, 128.726500 (at the Gatbawi Tourist Area parking lot)

HIKE DESCRIPTION

This hike lies 12 kilometers to the northeast of the Central Business District (CBD) of Korea's third largest city, Daegu, and takes in a high mountain ridge and two Buddhist temples at the start and end of the hike.

Begin the hike at the elegant Donghwasa Temple Complex and follow the well-marked trails toward the summit of Palgonsan (aka Mt. Palgong), which is a good 2-hour hike with steady elevation gain up to the ridgeline to the summit, about 4 kilometers from Donghwasa Temple.

Due to a large number of official buildings and towers atop the ridgeline at the summit, views can be slightly disappointing, but it's an impressive hike up to the top as you pass two smaller temples. Once the summit has been claimed, follow the ridgeline trail as it undulates across a rather rocky path in and out of scrub and small trees. A good midpoint landmark is

the Palgonsan Country Club golf course on the southern flanks of the mountain. After hiking about 6.5 kilometers from Palgonsan summit, you will reach a smaller peak at 997 meters, which lies nearly above the golf course.

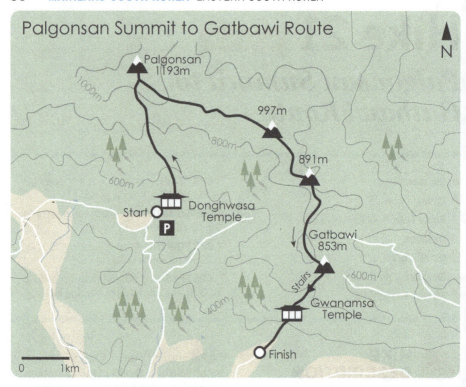

There are no huts or other tourist conveniences along this route. The trail is not heavily used, and as such, it is a great choice if you want some alone time in nature.

After some smaller peaks, the rocky summit of Gatbawi—home to the Gatbawi "Medicine" Buddha—will come into view about 45–60 minutes before you reach it. After arriving at Gatbawi and enjoying the temple and views, continue down the stairs (there are many of them!) as they descend toward the end point of the hike.

Hike 22 MODERATE

Mountain and Waterfall Double-Back Loop

🌐 **Location:** Juwangsan National Park, North Gyeongsang Province

⭐ **Rating:** Moderate

🥾 **Route Type:** Loop

📍 **Distance:** 16 km

🕐 **Duration:** 7–8 hr

⛰ **Elevation Gain:** 950 m

🍼 **Stroller Friendly:** No

🚩 **GPS START:** 36.390216, 129.141058 (at the parking lot)

📍 **GPS POINT:** 36.396387, 129.155950 (at the WC)

🔺 **GPS SUMMIT:** 36.389444, 129.162325 (at Juwangsan summit at 721 m)

🚩 **GPS FINISH:** 36.390216, 129.141058

HIKE DESCRIPTION

This full-day hike departs from Daejeong-sa Temple onto a ridgeline trail where you will bag three peaks—Janggunbong, Geumeungwangi, and finally, Juwangsan. The hike begins in the same way as Hike 17. However, after departing Daejeongsa Temple, you will bear to the left at the trail junction, cross a small bridge (on your immediate right after turning left), and follow the trail as it proceeds to the north. After a few minutes, you will encounter a series of stairs up and around the rocky outcrop that looms above. At the top, you will arrive at an observation deck overlooking the temple and approach road.

Continue uphill from the observation platform, following the trail in a northwesterly direction until you reach Janggunbong, the first of three summits on this hike, at 687 meters. From the summit marker, you will now change

to an easterly direction and follow the trail as it descends and then rises along a heavily forested ridgeline that traces the northern side of the river valley far below. According to a sign on this section of trail, a typhoon destroyed this part of the forest many years ago, and new growth is now repopulating the area. About 800 meters past the sign, you will come across a multi-trail junction and make your second summit on this hike, Geumeungwangi, at 812 meters.

From here, take the trail on your right and descend the steep mountainside to the southeast toward the valley floor, which lies 550 meters below. About halfway down, the trail joins up with a stream and follows it all the way to the valley floor. At the junction with the main valley floor trail, turn right and proceed on the main trail toward the southwest, enjoying the views and many waterfalls. When you reach the WC, turn around and use the bridge just upriver and then hike up the stairs to reach Juwangamsa

Hermitage Temple. Following your visit to the temple, take the trail to the northeast for 500 meters as it descends toward the river and crosses the main valley floor trail once again.

On the valley floor trail, backtrack in a northeasterly direction until you reach a bridge crossing the river on your right. Cross the bridge and follow the trail sign toward the summit of Juwangsan and Daejeongsa Temple. For the first kilometer, this trail follows a stream until you reach a trail on your right leading to the southwest. Take this new trail and begin the ascent up to the ridgeline, which runs along the south side of the valley.

After about 2.5 kilometers, you will come into a hilltop clearing at the third summit of the day, which is the namesake of the park—Juwangsan, at 721 meters. After a rest, descend along the ridgeline trail, merging with the main valley trail again about 200 meters from Daejeongsa Temple, which lies to your left. From the temple, backtrack along the paved roadway before ending at the parking lot.

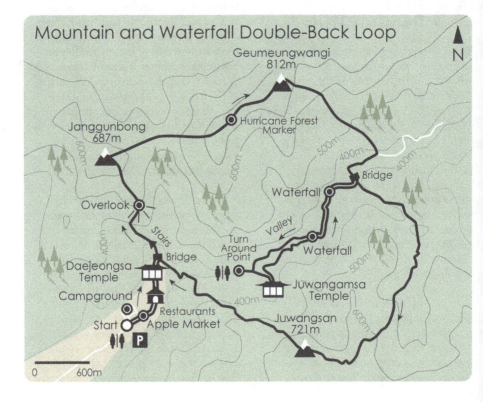

Mountain and Waterfall Double-Back Loop
N

Geumeungwangi 812m
Hurricane Forest Marker
Janggunbong 687m
Bridge
Waterfall
Overlook
Waterfall
Turn Around Point
Valley
Daejeongsa Temple
Bridge
Stairs
Campground
Juwangamsa Temple
Restaurants
Apple Market
Start
Juwangsan 721m
P

0   600m

Southern South Korea

N

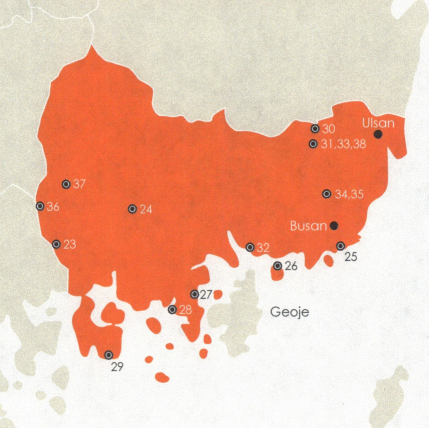

30
31,33,38
Ulsan
37
34,35
36
24
23
Busan
32
25
26
27
28
Geoje
29

Hike 23 EASY

Hadong History Park and River Overlook Route

🌐 **Location:** Hadong County, South Gyeongsang Province

⭐ **Rating:** Easy

🔄 **Route Type:** Out and Back

📏 **Distance:** 2.5 km

🕐 **Duration:** 2–4 hr (includes stops)

⛰️ **Elevation Gain:** 100 m

🛒 **Stroller Friendly:** No

📍 **GPS START:** 35.063469, 127.742647 (at the riverside parking lot)

🔺 **GPS SUMMIT:** 35.066740, 127.743628 (at the observatory tower)

📍 **GPS POINT:** 35.067985, 127.745256 (at the ROK Army War Memorial)

📍 **GPS POINT:** 35.069535, 127.742734 (at the gazebo/pavilion)

🏁 **GPS FINISH:** 35.063469, 127.742647

 **HIKE DESCRIPTION**

The town of Hadong lies just north of the main East-West Motorway 10, which crosses the ROK along its southern coastline. It also lies between the coastal watershed and the extensive estuary of the Seonjingang River near Gwangyang City and the south-facing foothills of the Jirisan National Park, where both green tea and persimmons are grown in abundance.

Start the hike at the large parking lot (which has a large WC at the northwestern end) that lies along the riverfront adjacent to a lovely pine tree forest park. Enjoy the huge sandy beach, which is set against the rolling green hills topped with temples and the Seomjingyo Bridge.

From the beach, proceed inland toward the town, crossing the white steel footbridge over the main road and following the steps up the hill for about 250 meters until you approach the base steps up to the observatory tower. From atop the tower there are photographic panels that point out the various mountains and river features along all cardinal points of the compass. From the base of the tower the views are also spectacular.

Continuing on, proceed in a northeasterly direction from the observatory tower, walking about 200 meters toward the ROK Army War Memorial, which also offers expansive views to the south over

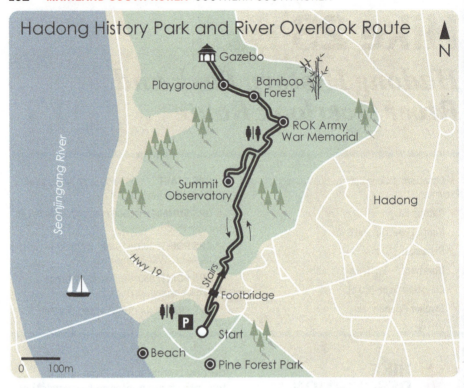

Hadong History Park and River Overlook Route

the town and across the agricultural fields to the railroad bridge. Along the route there is a WC and several benches and swings. From here, enjoy the ridgetop views to the north along the river valley with the mountains of Jirisan NP in the background.

From the memorial, you will now change direction and head in a northwesterly direction following the contour of the ridgeline as it dips and then rises along the pathway, passing a playground on the western side. Enjoy the serene "knocking" noises of the bamboo forest along the eastern side of the path.

The trail begins to rise toward the terminus of this route, which is found atop a hill in the form of a nice rectangular gazebo-style building with views to the west and over the river. From here, retrace your steps back to the parking lot to complete the hike.

Hike 24 `EASY`

Jinjuseong Riverwalk and Museum Loop

🌐 **Location:** Jinju, South Gyeongsang Province

⭐ **Rating:** Easy

〰️ **Route Type:** Loop

📏 **Distance:** 3 km

🕐 **Duration:** 2–3 hr (not including a visit to Jinju National Museum)

⛰️ **Elevation Gain:** 50 m

🛒 **Stroller Friendly:** Yes

🏁 **GPS START:** 35.190479, 128.080455 (at the parking lot)

🔺 **GPS SUMMIT:** 35.187125, 128.075321 (at the southeastern watchtower)

🚩 **GPS FINISH:** 35.190479, 128.080455

HIKE DESCRIPTION

Even if you don't like hiking, Jinju Fortress (Jinjuseong) is a must-see for its rich historical and cultural meaning to the Korean people. During the Japanese invasions (1592–1598), Korean forces at the Jinju Fortress successfully repelled the Japanese siege in 1592, only to be overcome in the summer of the following year after a hard-fought battle. Following the sacking of the fortress, nearly the entire population of Jinju and all defenders who were sheltered within its walls were put to the sword by the Japanese aggressors. Approximately 70,000 people perished, making this fortress truly hallowed ground for the Koreans.

Despite its grisly past, the fortress is now a peaceful park and tourist destination, offering paved trails (with some steps) and a few small hills with commanding views over the city and the river to the south. Many benches can be found along the pathways, and WCs are also available, making it an easy and convenient destination for parents to take young children.

Within the fortress are well-preserved and rebuilt gates, watchtowers, cannons, temples, and other historical markers, but the gem in the crown of the fortress is the

exceptionally well-designed and modern Jinju National Museum, which takes the visitor all the way back to prehistory up through the Japanese invasion. Note the museum's remarkable illustrations and photographs of the fortress from the past four centuries.

Beyond the museum, there are many other famous locations within the fortress walls, but one is particularly well known throughout all of Korea. Along the riverbank to the eastern side of the fortress lies the famous Uiam Bawi or "Rock of Righteousness." During the invasion period, a Korean woman named Nongae embraced one of the Japanese generals and then leapt from this rock into the river, taking both herself and the Japanese general to their deaths. A shrine and pavilion lie above the rock, offering a peaceful place to study and contemplate the heroic actions of this Korean patriot from long ago.

Hike 25 EASY

Igidae Park Coastal Trail Route

🌍 **Location:** Busan

⭐ **Rating:** Easy

〰️ **Route Type:** Point to Point (with the option for a loop hike)

👣 **Distance:** 4.7 km (11 km as a loop)

🕐 **Duration:** 2–3 hr (4–5 hr as a loop)

⛰️ **Elevation Gain:** 100 m (180 m as a loop)

🛒 **Stroller Friendly:** No

🚩 **GPS START:** 35.132059, 129.120437 (at the parking lot)

🔺 **GPS SUMMIT:** 35.117220, 129.121799 (210 m)

🚩 **GPS FINISH 1:** 35.100521, 129.124389 (at the Oryukdo Skywalk)

🚩 **GPS FINISH 2:** 35.130620, 129.119031 (200 m southwest of parking lot)

HIKE DESCRIPTION

The Igidae Park Coastal Trail is located in Busan, the second-largest city in Korea and a major maritime hub. The hike can be done as a one-way trip or in a loop. It offers fresh ocean breezes, rocky sea cliffs, and breathtaking views from the cliffs (fitted with stairs and footbridges, making the trail both exciting and accessible).

Start at the parking lot, pausing for a moment at the observation point to

gaze out upon Gwangan Bridge and modern towers, which dominate Busan across the bay. After enjoying the views, follow the trail to the east and then south as it drops down and around an imposing blue glass building, known as "The View." Head toward the rocky shoreline, where you will see the first of several footbridges spanning rocky sea gorges. Cross the first one and stay on the trail as it gains in elevation and takes you through several different coastal environments.

After about 3.5 kilometers, you will come across an observation platform that offers views to the south along rocky cliffs toward a formation of stacked rocks called Nongbawi. Passing this impressive viewpoint, the trail will head through the forest until you reach an observation point above a manicured park, to which you then descend by way of stairs. Once across the park, you will see a U-shaped glass walkway that extends beyond the rocky sea cliffs and directly over the crashing waves far below. This place is called the Oryukdo Skywalk—a favorite

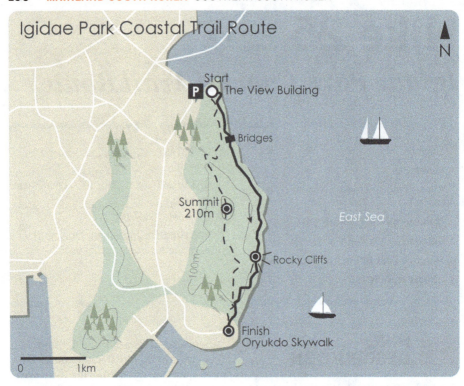

Igidae Park Coastal Trail Route

N

Start
P The View Building
Bridges
Summit 210m
East Sea
100 m
Rocky Cliffs
Finish
Oryukdo Skywalk
0   1km

among visitors. Once you have taken in the amazing views from the skywalk, return to the start point by taxi or bus.

Alternatively, backtrack all the way up the trail, crossing the park. You will reach a clear junction point with a trail continuing uphill toward the roadway (about 350 meters away) or toward the coastal trail, which you hiked earlier. Head for the roadway, and once you merge onto it, turn right and follow the sidewalk on the road for about 900 meters until you see a small parking lot with a large gazebo-style shelter on the hill just adjacent to it on the north side. Walk to the gazebo and then follow the trail north about 650 meters, climbing in elevation for about 90 meters until you emerge in a grassy field with a helipad and outdoor gym equipment.

Although the views are not spectacular from this high point on the loop, there are some glimpses back toward Busan and out to sea. Walk across the field heading north and descend into the forest. As you descend from the high point, you will come to a clearing about 500 meters down the trail, which offers better views and has a nice gazebo-style shelter. The trail will run about 1.3 kilometers until it turns sharply to the east for the last 200 meters and merges onto a road.

Back at the road junction, do a quick dogleg by turning right for 20 meters up the road, then turn left and cross the road. You will take the concrete road, which then turns to dirt after 100 meters toward the temple of Baeglyeonsa. Stay on the road and follow it all the way to the temple. Pass through the small temple and take the steep trail and stairs down to the road. Turn right and hike 200 meters to reach the parking lot.

Hike 26 EASY

Yeondaebong Summit Loop

🌐 **Location:** Gadeok Island

⭐ **Rating:** Easy

〰️ **Route Type:** Loop

👣 **Distance:** 4.8 km

🕐 **Duration:** 2–3 hr

⛰️ **Elevation Gain:** 300 m

🍼 **Stroller Friendly:** No

🚩 **GPS START:** 35.022681, 128.822467 (at the trailhead, just 100 m north of the parking lot)

🔺 **GPS SUMMIT:** 35.026636, 128.833992 (at Yeondaebong summit at 459 m)

🚩 **GPS FINISH:** 35.022681, 128.822467

 ## HIKE DESCRIPTION

Nearly everyone living on Geoje Island passes through Gadeok Island on the way to Busan and the mainland. It's not only the home of the Geoje Grand Bridge easternmost terminus, but also the western terminal of the massive Busan New Port container-handling facility. However, the small island of Gadeok has a long and rather dark history: it was once the home of two Japanese castles (wajo), and over 1,000

Japanese troops were garrisoned here during the 1592–1598 Japanese invasion (Imjin War).

From the trailhead, proceed on a well-groomed trail that increases in elevation, passing a gazebo shelter, until you reach the summit clearing of Yeondaebong at 459 meters. At this location, there are informational signs about the history of the area, as well as a rebuilt stone smoke tower. Enjoy views from the summit to the west toward Geoje Island and the Geoje Grand Bridge. Continuing on the trail past the summit, you will reach a clear junction after about 2.5 kilometers (as measured from the trailhead). Turn left and follow a concrete fire road downhill in a westerly direction until you emerge near the parking lot. **(Note: There are many trails on Gadeok Island, and it's easy to combine them into a long day hike if desired!)**

Note: At the Gadeok Rest Area, check out a small museum dedicated to the Geoje Grand Bridge.

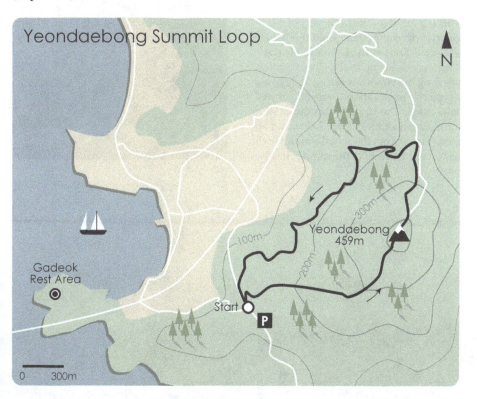

Hike 27 EASY

Cable Car to Mireuksan Summit

🌐 **Location:** Tongyeong, South Gyeongsang Province

⭐ **Rating:** Easy

🔗 **Route Type:** Out and Back

📏 **Distance:** 0.6 km (trail portion, return)

🕐 **Duration:** 1 hr

⛰️ **Elevation Gain:** 80 m (trail portion)

🛒 **Stroller Friendly:** No

🚩 **GPS START:** 34.826378, 128.425315 (at the Cable Car Station parking lot)

🔺 **GPS SUMMIT:** 34.810693, 128.415978 (at Mireuksan summit at 458 m)

🚩 **GPS FINISH:** 34.826378, 128.425315

HIKE DESCRIPTION

This is a fun day hike in the city of Tongyeong, sometimes called the "Venice of Korea." Start at the Lower Cable Car Station and ride up to the Upper Station, enjoying the views out across Tongyeong as you rise in elevation toward the top of Mireuksan. The Upper Cable Car Station terminates about 80 meters below and 300 meters away from the actual summit of the mountain. The trail to the summit involves

Cable Car to Mireuksan Summit

N

P
Start

100m

Cable Car

200m

Mireuksan
458m
360° Lookout

300m

0   300m

climbing many wooden staircases until you reach a broad observation platform.

From the summit platform, there are breathtaking views back toward Geoje and in all other directions, including the city and islands to the south-southwest. This is a very popular location for tourists, and this summit will often be packed with

people. If you wish to avoid the crowds, try visiting on a weekday morning.

To complete the hike, backtrack to the Upper Cable Car Station and take it back down to the Lower Station. Note that it is also possible to ride up and hike down if desired. Just take one of the many trails from the summit of this small mountain.

Hike 28 EASY

Saryang Island Ridgeline Route

🌐 **Location:** Saryang Island

⭐ **Rating:** Easy

🔀 **Route Type:** Point to Point

📏 **Distance:** 7.5 km

🕐 **Duration:** 4–5 hr

⛰ **Elevation Gain:** 400 m

🛒 **Stroller Friendly:** No

🚩 **GPS START:** 34.908595, 128.313880 (at the Tongyeong-Saryang Ferry Boat Terminal)

🚩 **GPS START:** 34.838121, 128.180837 (at the Donji Village bus stop)

🔺 **GPS SUMMIT:** 34.846024, 128.182516 (at Jirisan summit at 399 m)

🚩 **GPS FINISH:** 34.844386, 128.223114 (at the Jinchon Village Ferry Boat Terminal)

HIKE DESCRIPTION

This is a very special hike, not only because it's a beautiful trail with great views, but also for the ferry ride across the pristine waters between Tongyeong and Saryang Islands. Enjoy the slower pace of life on this offshore paradise, famous for seafood, garlic, and hiking!

Start at the ferry terminal in Tongyeong and take the 9:00 a.m. ferry. From there, it's a 40-minute ride to Saryang Island, passing through a peaceful but active waterway full of aquaculture operations

and fishing vessels hard at work. On arrival, depart the ferry and board the island bus, which is timed with the ferry's arrival. This is a popular hike for locals, so you will not be alone.

After a short ride of less than 10 minutes, depart at Donji Village. Follow the local hikers and start the hike from this point. Stop for a minute to gaze at the rocky ridgeline high above the village to the north, which is the summit peak where you are headed. Continuing on, follow the small signs north from the bus stop, passing houses on your right and rice paddies on your left for the first 200 meters. The houses will soon be replaced by fields and the signs will point more to the northwest, and then the fields end, and you will enter the forest trail proper. The elevation climbs quickly, and along both sides of the trail you'll see stone statues and other carvings. The trail soon breaks out of the forest onto a rocky ridgeline with truly awe-inspiring views across the island, sea, and back toward the mainland. After scrambling across the rocky ridgeline trail, you will soon arrive at the

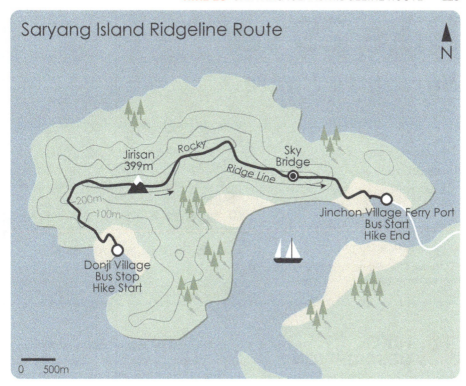

Saryang Island Ridgeline Route

N

Jirisan
399m

Rocky

Ridge Line

Sky
Bridge

200m

100m

Jinchon Village Ferry Port
Bus Start
Hike End

Donji Village
Bus Stop
Hike Start

0   500m

summit marker for the Jirisan summit at 399 meters (not to be confused with the similarly named Jirisan National Park on the mainland).

Head out from the summit and continue on the trail heading toward the east. The trail drops in elevation about 50 meters, and after 1.2 kilometers, you will arrive at a four-way junction with a small outdoor "snack bar" offering simple snacks and homemade makkoli rice wine. Continue straight in an eastward direction after enjoying a rest and some of the local fare.

Proceeding on, you will reach a minor summit within about 750 meters, and then the path will bear to the south and turn eastward again. There are a few lone trails running to the north and south off the main ridgeline trail, but stay on the main trail, which is clearly marked and obvious due to heavy usage. The next stretch offers many sharp rocky

stretches where you will want to be careful while enjoying exhilarating views on both sides of the knife-edge trail. The trail becomes a series of stairs and steep ascents and descents among granite spires until you reach a cable-stayed suspension footbridge, aptly named the "Sky Bridge," which links two rocky outcrops across a deep chasm far below. From the bridge, there are spectacular views toward the town with the ferry port clearly visible, along with the newly completed vehicle bridge linking Saryang Island with Hado Island to the south.

After enjoying the views from atop this spectacular bridge, continue on the trail as it begins the steep descent down to the harbor front, where you can arrive in time to catch the 4:00 p.m. ferry back to Tongyeong. As the ferry pulls away from the pier, turn around and gaze at the long, high ridge that you just conquered.

Hike 29 EASY

Boriamsa Route

- 🌐 **Location:** Namhae Island
- ⭐ **Rating:** Easy
- 〰️ **Route Type:** Out and Back
- 📍 **Distance:** 2.5 km
- 🕐 **Duration:** 2–3 hr
- ⛰️ **Elevation Gain:** 150 m
- 🍼 **Stroller Friendly:** Yes (except for some stairs just near the temple)

- 🚩 **GPS START:** 34.754973, 127.991613 (at the parking lot)
- 🔺 **GPS SUMMIT:** 34.755203, 127.982912 (at Geumsan summit at 705 m)
- 🏠 **GPS TEMPLE:** 34.752161, 127.983244 (at Boriamsa Temple)
- 🏁 **GPS FINISH:** 34.754973, 127.991613

HIKE DESCRIPTION

On this hike, you will visit Namhae, a sister island to the west of Geoje, accessible from the mainland by bridge. After arriving at the start point in the parking lot, proceed to the west following the well-marked trail toward the temple. After about 900 meters, you will reach a series of steps that descend to the temple. At this point, there is also a trail that leads to the summit only 300 meters away. It is a worthwhile side trip; however, the views from the temple are better than from the summit. Having bagged the peak, descend to the temple and take your time enjoying the views from a number of different observation platforms and levels within the complex, which is built upon a large

Boriamsa Route

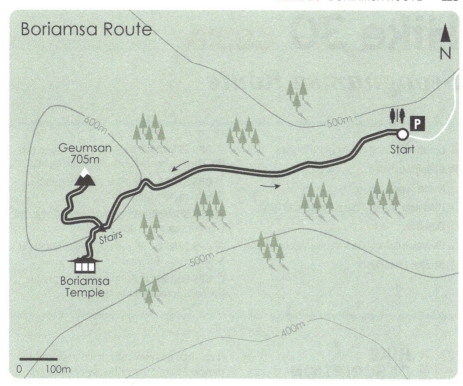

N

600m

Geumsan
705m

500m

Start

P

Stairs

500m

Boriamsa
Temple

400m

0   100m

granite outcrop just below the top of the mountain.

Following a relaxing visit to the temple, backtrack to the parking lot to complete this hike.

Note: There is a WC at both the parking lot and at the temple.

Hike 30 MODERATE

Seongnamsa Route

🌐 **Location:** Gajisan Provincial Park, Ulsan

⭐ **Rating:** Moderate

📿 **Route Type:** Loop

🧭 **Distance:** 10.5 km (alternative loop 13 km)

🕐 **Duration:** 6–8 hr

⛰️ **Elevation Gain:** 650 m (alternative loop 900 m)

🛒 **Stroller Friendly:** No

🚩 **GPS START:** 35.607946, 129.025848 (at the Hwy 24 tunnel entrance parking lot)

🚩 **GPS START:** 35.616520, 129.039253 (at the alternative footpath)

🔺 **GPS SUMMIT:** 35.620340, 129.002792 (at Gajisan summit at 1,241 m)

🏠 **GPS TEMPLE:** 35.621186, 129.032339 (at Seongnamsa Temple)

🚩 **GPS FINISH:** 35.617715, 129.039742 (at the restaurant parking area)

📖 HIKE DESCRIPTION

Gajisan is a rocky peak in the Yeongnam Alps with unobstructed 360-degree views. The hike follows a well-defined ridgeline trail, from which you can see the Seongnamsa Temple far below. Constructed in AD 824, Seongnamsa Temple is an active Buddhist Nunnery. This hike also includes several "makkoli huts" where rustic mountain culture can be enjoyed alongside common hiking

fare, such as spicy tofu, fried vegetable pancakes, and the milky, sweet rice wine known as makkoli.

There are two ways of proceeding on this hike: 1) the primary point to point route, or 2) an alternative footpath loop, which connects the parking lot just opposite from the "finish" point back toward the "start" point. The footpath is often closed for repairs, so I offer the point to point as the primary route.

Begin at the small parking lot on the left-hand side of the road just before the tunnel on Hwy 24. Cross the highway and proceed to climb the staircase on the opposite side of the road. At the top of the steps, merge onto the trail and turn right toward Gajisan, following the trail signs.

Continue on this trail as it rises over 650 meters up to the rocky summit of Gajisan about 3.1 kilometers ahead. En route to the summit, you will pass the first of three makkoli huts. At the summit, enjoy the options at another makkoli hut as well as

the grand panorama that stretches out before you all the way to the horizon in nearly all directions.

After bagging this peak, continue on the trail, heading in a northeasterly direction for another 30–40 minutes until you reach a fire road adjacent to a viewpoint just below a large cliff face. After taking in the view, you will pass the final makkoli hut within 100 meters.

Continue on the fire road heading in a roughly eastward direction. You will pass one footpath, then take the second footpath (in the vicinity of 35.632418, 129.034532), which heads steeply down the mountain in a southbound direction toward the temple. **(Note: The temple is visible from many spots along the ridgeline. Be careful not to follow the fire road if it passes over the ridge to the northeast, as it will lead in the wrong direction, away from the temple.)**

Take a right turn off the road and follow the trail steeply downhill toward the temple. Continue the descent until you emerge onto a paved road in the temple vicinity. Turn right and proceed to the temple, crossing a stone footbridge. Soon you will enter the main courtyard where you'll see a three-tiered pagoda and several other cultural relics.

After enjoying this retreat, exit the temple and follow the creek downstream along the paved path until it emerges onto the main road, with the parking lot and restaurants across the road where the hike finish point is located.

Note: In the autumn, this is a really spectacular location to enjoy the changing colors of the forest canopy.

Hike 31 `MODERATE`

Eastern Route to Valley Floor

🌐 **Location:** Yeongnam Alps, Ulsan

⭐ **Rating:** Moderate

🔀 **Route Type:** Point to Point

📍 **Distance:** 16.5 km

🕐 **Duration:** 7–8 hr

⛰ **Elevation Gain:** 800 m

🛒 **Stroller Friendly:** No

🚩 **GPS START:** 35.580598, 129.027557 (at the parking lot above Hwy 69 tunnel)

🔺 **GPS SUMMIT:** 35.516123, 129.052598 (at Yeongchuksan summit at 1,081 m)

🚩 **GPS FINISH:** 35.523214, 129.008374 (at the bus stop along Hwy 69)

HIKE DESCRIPTION

This hike takes in four peaks (three of which are over 1,000 meters in elevation) by way of a high mountain ridge that runs along the eastern side of the deep valley. **(Note: Only the peaks over 1,000 meters are discussed in this hike: Ganwolsan, Sinbulsan, and Yeongchuksan.)** The views over the Yeongnam Alps toward the East Sea, the city of Ulsan, and the petrochemical complex of Onsan are spectacular on a clear day. There is one well-stocked mountain hut at the midpoint of the hike, which offers hot meals and a nice WC, as well as camping options for those interested in staying the night.

Begin the hike at the public parking lot built above the northern pass leading into the valley. From here, head in an easterly direction and follow the trail markers up into the forest. This trail rises rapidly in elevation to the first peak, Ganwolsan, and then steadies out with some undula-

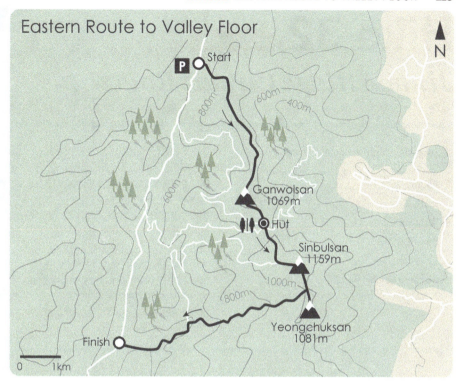

Eastern Route to Valley Floor

N

P ○ Start

Ganwolsan
1069m

Hut

Sinbulsan
1159m

Yeongchuksan
1081m

Finish ○

0   1km

tions as it continues along the ridgeline. You'll find there are many rocky outcrops from which to enjoy the views. After bagging Ganwolsan, the trail descends to the Ganwoljae Hut, where a mountain pass road crosses the ridge at a saddle.

Once refreshed, continue in a southbound direction and again begin to climb in elevation toward Sinbulsan. In the distance, you should be able to see the high point for today's hike, Yeongchuksan, 2.3 kilometers away. Continue on the path to reach the summit of Yeongchuksan, from which a large portion of Southeast Korea will lie below you, with the silhouettes of gray and blue "mountains behind mountains" stretching north, west, and south, and the sparkling East Sea shining a deep blue to the east.

After bagging Yeongchuksan, you will now backtrack toward Sinbulsan. About 700 meters before reaching that peak, turn to the left and take the well-marked trail to the east back toward the valley floor and Hwy 69. This trail descends steeply for about 5 kilometers, opening onto a road after the first 3 kilometers. For the final 2 kilometers of the hike, you will pass village homes and holiday pensions until you reach the bus stop, where you can either catch a northbound bus (328) back to the start point or hail a taxi at one of the shops or restaurants in the area.

Hike 32 MODERATE

Jinhae Ridge Circuit Route

🌐 **Location:** Jinhae City, South Gyeongsang Province

⭐ **Rating:** Moderate

🥾 **Route Type:** Point to Point

🧭 **Distance:** 24 km

🕐 **Duration:** 7–8 hr

🏔 **Elevation Gain:** 700 m

🛒 **Stroller Friendly:** No

🚩 **GPS START:** 35.120142, 128.715972 (at the parking lot)

📍 **GPS POINT:** 35.142951, 128.735246 (at Bear Mountain summit)

🔺 **GPS SUMMIT:** 35.155101, 128.738460 (at Woongsan summit at 708 m)

📍 **GPS POINT:** 35.169398, 128.700415 (at Anmin Pass Tunnel, trail crossover point)

📍 **GPS POINT:** 35.173314, 128.678383 (at second platform gazebo shelter)

🚩 **GPS FINISH:** 35.156342, 128.674768 (in the vicinity of this location)

HIKE DESCRIPTION

Jinhae (aka Chinhae) is a bustling port city famous for its large ROK Naval Base and Naval Academy. The city is tightly packed around the port area and ringed by mountains on all sides, except for the south where the sea meets the shore.

This hike begins at a parking lot on the main highway into Jinhae (Hwy 2/77), on the crest of a hill about 900 meters southeast of STX Shipyard. Although the hike is long, the trail conditions are generally very good, and much of it follows well-defined roadways. This hike does not demand too much exertion, just stamina!

Start the hike by proceeding toward the white steel footbridge crossing the highway. Take the road, which starts to climb up into the forest, following the trail markers toward Bear Mountain. Due to the large number of trails in the

area, just continue to follow those that are most trodden and continue to increase in elevation. They will all converge together, and soon you'll pass a mobile phone tower. Continue on the rocky trail as it darts along rocks and through the trees until you reach an opening in the forest and get your first good look at the rocky spire of Bear Mountain rising above you.

The spectacular view of this rocky outcrop, similar to a thumb sticking out of the ridgeline, is only matched by the serpentine network of stairs and platforms constructed to access it from the trail below. Once at the top of the stairs, enjoy a well-earned rest and the view across all of Jinhae City far below. Keep a keen eye out for naval vessels in the harbor and channel to the south.

Depart Bear Mountain, heading in a northerly direction. About 1.5 kilometers farther up the trail (after a slight increase in elevation), you will find a small rocky

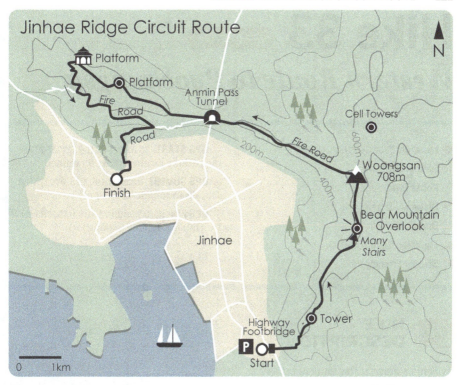

Jinhae Ridge Circuit Route

N

Platform

Platform

Fire Road

Road

Road

Anmin Pass Tunnel

200m

Fire Road

400m

600m

Cell Towers

Woongsan 708m

Bear Mountain Overlook

Many Stairs

Finish

Jinhae

Highway Footbridge

Tower

P Start

0   1km

area with a summit marker showing 708 meters; this is the high point for the day's hike. At this point, follow the trail as it becomes a fire road and turns sharply to the west, and continue to follow the ridgeline as it descends toward Anmin Pass. When you reach the pass, just below you will be a small local road with a tunnel and parking lots. You'll find a WC and an observation platform where you can admire Jinhae from a different perspective.

Backtrack to the trail and continue in a westerly direction. Soon the trail will begin to increase in elevation once again, and the first of two wooden platforms come into view. Climb to the top of the first one to enjoy the 360-degree views and marvel at the large manufacturing city of Changwon to the north, with rows upon rows of green-roofed factories. Continue on the rocky ridgeline trail until you reach a second platform and gazebo shelter. After taking a rest, continue on

the trail for less than 50 meters until you reach a junction where trails continue in all directions. Turn left and take the trail descending toward Jinhae to the south.

Follow this trail through the forest for about 1 kilometer until you emerge onto a concrete fire road. Turn left and proceed downhill, following the road until it merges with a paved main road, then turn right and follow Anmingogae-gil Road, which is famous for the Jinhae cherry blossoms that bloom all along its length in the springtime. Eventually you will emerge in the northern suburbs of Jinhae, where you can get a snack at a convenience store and call a taxi to return to the starting point.

Note: This hike can be shortened considerably by just hiking the first half as described, and then taking a taxi from the Anmin Pass tunnel crossing location parking lot back to Jinhae City and the start point.

Hike 33 MODERATE

Western Route to Pyochungsa

🌐 **Location:** Yeongnam Alps, Ulsan

⭐ **Rating:** Moderate

〰 **Route Type:** Point to Point

📍 **Distance:** 11.5 km

🕐 **Duration:** 5–7 hr

⛰ **Elevation Gain:** 700 m

👶 **Stroller Friendly:** No

🚩 **GPS START:** 35.580598, 129.027557 (at the parking lot above Hwy 69 tunnel)

🔺 **GPS SUMMIT:** 35.558006, 128.972175 (at Jaeyaksan summit at 1,189 m)

🚩 **GPS FINISH:** 35.532327, 128.955758 (at Pyochungsa Temple parking lot)

HIKE DESCRIPTION

This hike starts at the same point as Hikes 31 and 38; however, for this hike you will head to the western end of the parking lot and take the trail up into the forest. The western route is both shorter and less intimidating than the eastern route, as only one main peak is encountered. This hike will take in the western ridgeline high above the valley and several large fields of "silver reeds," with views for many kilometers from the grassy peak. The trail is split between fire road and footpath but is clearly marked throughout, and there are opportunities for refreshments along the way at several small restaurants past the large cable car station.

After reaching the summit, turn to the southeast until you reach a large clearing with roads. A trail marker here shows the way down to the southwest. You will descend following a stream bed past several tall waterfalls. A few of the falls (named Cheungcheung and Geumgang) are approximately 20 meters in height!

You will soon arrive at the magnificent ninth-century AD Pyochunsa Temple Complex. Following a tour of this temple, continue toward the parking lot about 400 meters to the west.

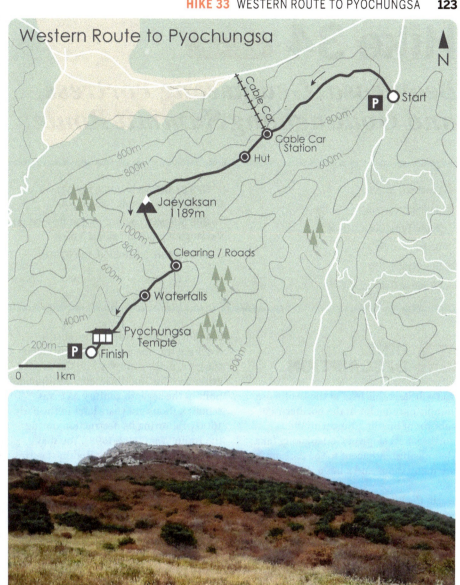

Western Route to Pyochungsa

N

Cable Car

P Start

Cable Car Station

Hut

800m

600m

600m

800m

Jaeyaksan 1189m

1000m

800m

Clearing / Roads

600m

Waterfalls

400m

200m

Pyochungsa Temple

P Finish

800m

0   1km

Hike 34 MODERATE

Beomeosa, Geumseong Fortress, and Godangbong Summit Route

- 🌐 **Location:** Busan
- ⭐ **Rating:** Moderate
- 🔀 **Route Type:** Out and Back
- 📏 **Distance:** 6 km
- 🕐 **Duration:** 5–6 hr
- 🏔 **Elevation Gain:** 550 m

- 🚩 **GPS START:** 35.282268, 129.073112 (at the Beomeosa Temple parking lot)
- 🔺 **GPS SUMMIT:** 35.280341, 129.050404 (at Godangbong summit at 801.5 m)
- 🚩 **GPS FINISH:** 35.282268, 129.073112

HIKE DESCRIPTION

You will start this hike at the Beomeosa Temple parking lot in the northern suburbs of bustling Busan on the northeastern slope of Godangbong (aka Geumjeong). Adjacent to the parking lot are many shops and a large WC facility.

Begin the hike by proceeding uphill toward the temple in a northerly direction, which after 200 meters heads to the west and follows the main temple road for another 400 meters until reaching the first gate. Passing through the gate, make your way into the temple grounds. This Buddhist temple, originally built in the seventh century AD, was rebuilt a thousand years later in the early 1600s, following its destruction during the Imjin War (1592–1598). You may catch the monks reciting Buddhist sutras and burning incense. Proceed toward the "Temple Stay" side of the complex, then head south from the main courtyard along the road to a large double gate with a "guardian" holding an upraised sword depicted on it.

Pass through the gate and then bear to your right, following the well-marked road and trail toward the North Gate of Geumseong Fortress (aka Geumjeong-sanseong). This trail will start by crossing a rather rocky creek bed, but the trail will smooth out and the forest hike will begin in earnest. About 1.8 kilometers from the temple, you will pass a WC on your left and then 100 meters ahead you'll see the North Gate of Geumseong Fortress and the reconstructed stone wall, which runs to the northwest and southeast.

After reading the historical marker adjacent to the gate, pass through the gate and enter the fortress grounds. Turn right and follow the well-marked trail heading along the stone wall in a northwesterly direction. Stop after 150 meters at the small Exhibit Building on your left-hand side. This exhibit is about the Korean team that climbed Everest in the 1990s. There is also a WC at this location.

Depart the exhibit and continue on the trail as you gain elevation and pass

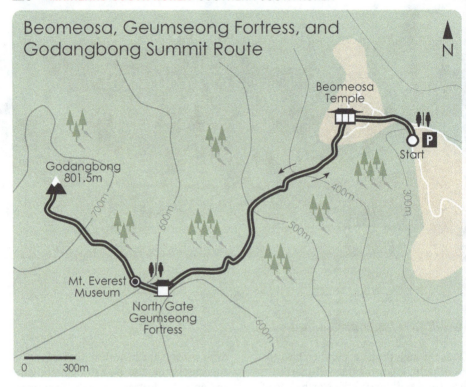

Beomeosa, Geumseong Fortress, and Godangbong Summit Route

N

Beomeosa Temple

Start

Godangbong
801.5m

700m
600m
500m
400m
300m

Mt. Everest
Museum

North Gate
Geumseong
Fortress

600m

0   300m

a natural spring (good for refilling canteens). The final 200 meters to the rocky summit of Godangbong include several steps and platforms affixed to the rocky peak, all of which offer amazing views toward downtown Busan and the fertile Gimhae Valley, full of rice and vegetable farms. Once on the final stairs, you will need to scramble a short distance to the stone marker to claim the summit at 801.5 meters. Backtrack to the parking lot to complete this amazing hike.

Hike 35 MODERATE

Beomeosa, Geumseong Fortress, and Botanical Gardens Route

- 🌐 **Location:** Busan
- ⭐ **Rating:** Moderate
- 🥾 **Route Type:** Point to Point
- 📏 **Distance:** 12.5 km
- 🕐 **Duration:** 5–6 hr
- ⛰ **Elevation Gain:** 550 m
- 🚼 **Stroller Friendly:** No

🚩 **GPS START:** 35.282268, 129.073112 (at the Beomeosa Temple parking lot)

📍 **GPS POINT:** 35.275471, 129.057469 (at the Geumseong Fortress North Gate)

📍 **GPS POINT:** 35.245460, 129.063697 (at the Geumseong Fortress East Gate)

📍 **GPS POINT:** 35.230048, 129.056806 (at the Geumseong Fortress South Gate)

🚩 **GPS FINISH:** 35.218850, 129.076137 (at Busan Botanical Gardens)

 ## HIKE DESCRIPTION

This hike begins at the same location as Hike 34, taking in the ruins of Geumseong, one of Korea's largest fortresses. Fun fact: The fortress's walled circumference was longer than 17 kilometers in the early 1700s.

As in Hike 34, proceed from Beomeosa Temple to the fortress's North Gate, and then turn left and head in a southerly direction, following the trail along the inside perimeter of the stone and earthwork walls as it skirts along a rocky edge of the mountaintop. At frequent intervals, rebuilt watchtowers and similar historical markers reveal the splendors of this once mighty fortress. Pass through the fully rebuilt South Gate and follow the trail that descends to the Busan Botanical Gardens. **(Note: There are restaurants near the upper cable car station just adjacent to the**

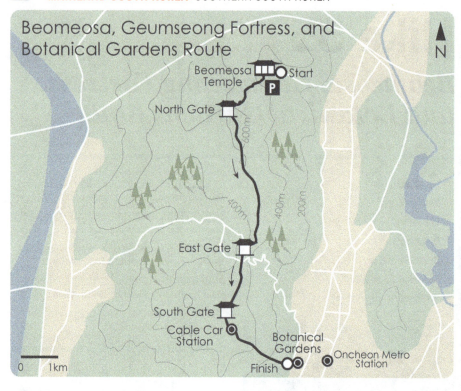

Beomeosa, Geumseong Fortress, and
Botanical Gardens Route

N

Beomeosa Temple
Start
North Gate
600m
400m
400m
200m
East Gate
South Gate
Cable Car Station
Botanical Gardens
Oncheon Metro Station
Finish

0   1km

South Gate. The spicy tofu is highly recommended!)

Back on the trail, about halfway down the mountain from the South Gate, keep an eye out for a large rocky outcrop with a cave, where you'll find a Buddhist shrine lit with candles. At the conclusion of the hike, a taxi can be hailed from the entrance of the Botanical Gardens to ferry you back to the start point at the Beomeosa Temple parking lot.

Hike 36 `DIFFICULT`

Twin Peaks Southwestern Route

🌐 **Location:** Jirisan National Park, South Jeolla Province

⭐ **Rating:** Difficult

👣 **Route Type:** Point to Point

🧭 **Distance:** 26 km

🕐 **Duration:** 11–12 hr

⛰ **Elevation Gain:** 1,600 m

🛏 **Stroller Friendly:** No

📍 **GPS START:** 35.254280, 127.496128 (at the Hwaeomsa Temple parking lot)

🔺 **GPS SUMMIT:** 35.293793, 127.532172 (at Nogodan summit at 1,507 m)

🔺 **GPS SUMMIT:** 35.316356, 127.569474 (at Banyabong summit at 1,732 m)

🚩 **GPS FINISH:** 35.264396, 127.583788 (at the Jikjeon Village parking lot)

HIKE DESCRIPTION

This full-day hike takes you to the famous Hwaeomsa Temple (established in AD 544) and to the summits of Nogodan and Banyabong. The descent is made via Piagol Valley to the small tourist town of Jikjeon.

You will start this hike at the temple parking lot where a WC is available. Heading in a northerly direction, take the staircase at the end of the parking lot into the Hwaeomsa Temple Complex and hike up to the main Gakhwangjeon Hall to admire the many Korean National Treasures housed here. Adjacent to the Gakhwangjeon, you'll find Korean National Treasure No. 12: a carved stone lantern standing proudly at 6.4 meters high. Take in the smell of incense and the sound of chanting, as well as the sight of the large golden Buddhas.

Depart the temple by backtracking toward the entrance, and then cross the stone bridge across the stream. Turn left and follow the trail, which is marked with a signboard. From here, the trail will rise in elevation through a lush, forested valley to the top of the main Jirisan east-west mountain ridgeline. The distance from Hwaeomsa to the ridgeline is about 6 kilometers and adds nearly 1,100 meters in elevation gain, so you will get a good workout on this stretch of trail.

Turn right, following the road and marked trail shortcut to the mountain hut. **(Note: See Hike 7 for more details in and around this area.)** Following a rest, take the trail from the hut as it rises past royal azalea bushes, proceeding to your first summit of the day, Nogodan, at 1,507 meters. From the summit, descend back down the walkway until you see the main ridgeline trail marker, and proceed in an easterly direction.

You will now hike the undulating ridgeline trail, enjoying the magnificent views to the north and south as you head toward Banyabong about 5.5 kilometers away. Note that approximately halfway to

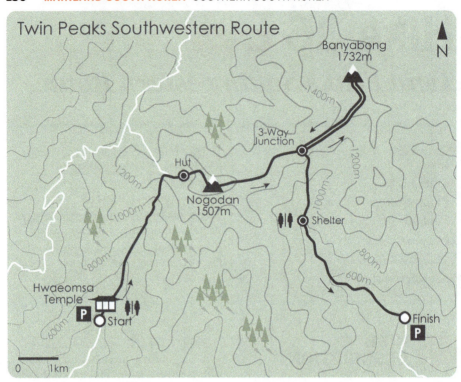

Twin Peaks Southwestern Route

Banyabong
1732m

N

3-Way
Junction

Hut

Nogodan
1507m

Shelter

Hwaeomsa
Temple

P
Start

Finish
P

0   1km

the second summit lies a clearly marked trail descending the southern slope of the mountainside. This is the three-way junction that you will return to once you bag Banyabong.

Push up the ridgeline spur in a northerly direction for about 1 kilometer until you reach Banyabong at 1,732 meters. On a clear day, Cheonwangbong (1,915 meters to the east) is clearly visible, as is Nogodan. There is a large rocky bald where you can rest a moment while soaking in the sunshine. Only a squirrel foraging in the low bushes nearby or a hawk wheeling high above on a thermal will take notice of you.

Depart this summit and backtrack all the way to the three-way junction. Turn left as you depart the ridgeline in a southerly direction and start your long descent toward the finish point in the Piagol Valley below. After about 2

kilometers on the trail, you will come across a rocky mountain stream, which you will follow for the rest of the hike as you descend through the valley. After another kilometer, you will come to a shelter and WC. At this point, you have already descended approximately 600 meters. Continue in a southeasterly direction, following the stream bed to the finish point in the tourist village about 4 kilometers away.

Note: The Piagol Valley is incredibly busy in the prime weeks of autumn. Thousands of day-trippers from across the country come to the valley to enjoy the fall color. Make sure to consider the popularity of this area when planning your trip if you wish not to be hampered by incessant crowds during peak tourist season.

Hike 37 `DIFFICULT`

Cheonwangbong Summit Southeastern Loop

🌐 **Location:** Jirisan National Park, South Gyeongsang Province

⭐ **Rating:** Difficult

🔄 **Route Type:** Loop

📏 **Distance:** 19 km

🕐 **Duration:** 9–10 hr

⛰ **Elevation Gain:** 1,450 m

🛒 **Stroller Friendly:** No

🚩 **GPS START:** 35.292883, 127.754220 (at the parking lot adjacent to the post office)

📍 **GPS POINT:** 35.332576, 127.716442 (at Jangteomok shelter)

🔺 **GPS SUMMIT:** 35.337016, 127.730593 (at Cheonwangbong summit at 1,915 m)

🚩 **GPS FINISH:** 35.292883, 127.754220

HIKE DESCRIPTION

This classic high-altitude hike takes you up Cheonwangbong (1,915 meters), the highest point on the peninsula within the ROK. Because of this hike's popularity, there will be lots of other hikers on this trail. At peak times, expect a 20-minute line to get a photo with the summit marker.

Start this hike at the main parking lot in the southeast of Jirisan National Park adjacent to the Korea Post Office. Set off toward the northern end of the lot and take the small, paved road that leads north between the buildings until it merges onto a larger paved road. At the junction, turn right onto the sidewalk and hike about 1.6 kilometers until you cross a bridge over a rocky mountain stream bed. After crossing the bridge, you will see a sign on your left at the trailhead. Take this trail.

Follow along the path of the rocky stream bed. After 1.2 kilometers, you will come

to a junction point where the trail to the right heads straight to the summit and the trail to the left heads toward the Jangteomok shelter. For this hike, bear left and stay on the trail headed toward the shelter, which is about 3.7 kilometers away. The trail begins to increase in elevation considerably, and the final hour before the ridgeline consists of unrelenting stairs, which will test even the fittest of hikers. Just as you approach the ridgeline and shelter, you will pass a natural spring on your right where you can fill up your water bottle.

Arriving at the Jangteomok shelter, you will have a variety of places to rest and refuel. The shelter also offers accommodation and sells simple fare. Mountain shelters on popular routes in Korea are a microcosm of Korea itself, where folks of all walks are drawn together by their love of nature, adventure, and comradery.

Getting back on the trail, head in a northeasterly direction following the

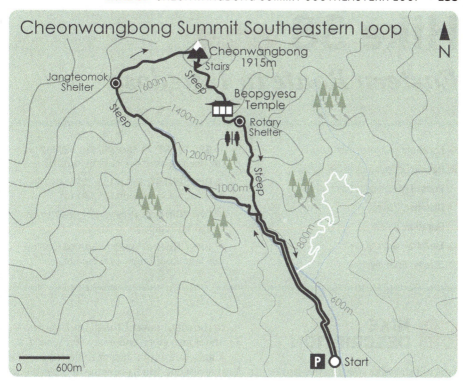

ridgeline trail toward the summit, which lies 1.4 kilometers away. At a few rocky outcrops, you will have a chance to finally put eyes on the prize as the summit gets closer and closer. Soon you will scale the last rocky rise, encountering a flat area at the top with the invariable hiking clubs taking group photos with banners and flags. After a final 10-meter scramble to the top of the rocky nub, you've claimed the summit! On clear days, all of Korea spreads out below you in all directions from this vantage point.

Once you have had your fill, proceed down the rocky trail to the east about 25 meters and take the trail on your right, which descends a series of steep stairs toward the rotary shelter. Fortunately, there are two places to take a rest during the incessantly steep descent: first, the lovely hermitage temple of Beopgyesa; and second, the small rotary shelter, which has a WC. Do take some time to explore the temple and climb up to its highest point to enjoy the view over the tiled temple buildings to the valley beyond.

Departing the temple, you will soon arrive at the nearby rotary shelter. From here, the next stretch of trail is quite steep once again and there are no places to rest, so make sure to do it now before continuing downhill.

Follow the trail steeply through the forest until you reach the familiar junction point. From here, backtrack all the way to the start point. Well done!

Hike 38 DIFFICULT

Eastern Route to Tongdosa

 Location: Yeongnam Alps, Ulsan

★ **Rating:** Difficult (due to the distance)

Route Type: Point to Point

Distance: 23 km

Duration: 8–9 hr

Elevation Gain: 900 m

Stroller Friendly: No

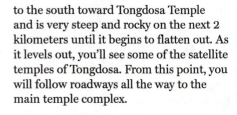

GPS START: 35.580598, 129.027557 (at the parking lot above Hwy 69 tunnel)

GPS SUMMIT: 35.516123, 129.052598 (at Yeongchuksan summit at 1,081 m)

GPS POINT: 35.487879, 129.064704 (at Tongdosa Temple)

GPS FINISH: 35.494273, 129.081226 (at the Tongdosa Temple parking Lot)

HIKE DESCRIPTION

This full-day hike starts in the same manner as Hike 31. However, upon reaching the rocky summit of Yeongchuksan, you will head downhill to the west (not east) about 100 meters until you come to a trail sign. This trail descends

to the south toward Tongdosa Temple and is very steep and rocky on the next 2 kilometers until it begins to flatten out. As it levels out, you'll see some of the satellite temples of Tongdosa. From this point, you will follow roadways all the way to the main temple complex.

After passing a satellite temple, you will continue about 2.5 kilometers on nearly flat roads. You'll see rice paddies and fields of chili peppers before arriving at the Tongdosa main temple complex. This large and venerable temple, from the seventh century AD, is one of the "Three Jewel Temples" of Korea and houses relics of the Buddha in a series of stupas (the "Diamond Altar") behind the main hall (Daeungjeon).

Having enjoyed the temple and, if time allows, its museum, continue on the final stretch of this hike as it proceeds along the wide path adorned with graceful elder pines, following a rocky stream bed in a northeasterly direction for the final 1.5 kilometers. You will complete the hike at the large public parking lot and adjacent tourist village.

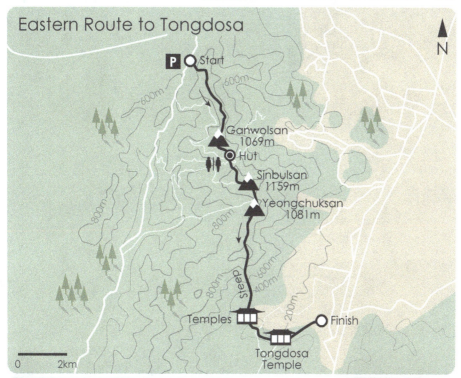

Eastern Route to Tongdosa

P O Start
600m
600m
Ganwolsan
1069m
O Hut
Sinbulsan
1159m
Yeongchuksan
1081m
800m
800m
600m
steep
400m
200m
Temples
Finish
Tongdosa
Temple

0   2km

N

Part III

Geoje Island

North Geoje

N

◎ 46

◎ 45

◎ 47,50,59,69

◎ 58

◎ 48

◎ 49

◎ 44

◎ 64,68

Geoje City

◎ 43

◎ 52   ◎ 51

56,57,67 ◎ ● ◎ 39   60,61   ◎ 53
        ◎ 40,42 62,63

◎ 41

◎ 54

◎ 65,66   ◎ 55

Camelia Island

Hike 39 `EASY`

Gohyeon Fortress Loop

⭐ **Rating:** Easy

🔁 **Route Type:** Loop

📍 **Distance:** 850 m

🕐 **Duration:** 20–60 min

⛰ **Elevation Gain:** 20 m

🛒 **Stroller Friendly:** Yes

🚩 **GPS START:** 34.88223, 128.6210

🔺 **GPS SUMMIT:** 34.88045, 128.6206 (at the carp pond)

🚩 **GPS FINISH:** 34.88223, 128.6210

 ## HIKE DESCRIPTION

This hike is a little loop along the fortress walls that surround current-day Geoje City Hall. Since 1453, Gohyeonseong has been both a seat of government and a defensive fortress. More recently it has been used as a command post enclosure of a POW camp during the Korean War (1950–1953).

The hike starts at the corner of the main road at the historical marker that describes the history of the fortress. Next, proceed up the short but steep paved red path toward the gate. Continue along the pathway to the carp pond. Ample shade makes this a lovely stop during a hot summer day. Children will enjoy seeing the carp and the butterflies, frogs, and other inhabitants of this little pond. Continuing around the loop, you'll find a picnic area with benches, ample shade, and an open grassy area. After a rest, continue down the hill past the parking lot to the main road and turn left onto the sidewalk where you can walk back to the starting point.

The route is completely paved, and there is minimal elevation gain and plenty of places to take a rest. As an added benefit, there is a nearby convenience store just across the street from the main entrance of the city hall.

Hike 40 EASY

Gohyeon Riverwalk Loop

★ **Rating:** Easy

⌇ **Route Type:** Loop

📍 **Distance:** 2 km

🕐 **Duration:** 1 hr

⛰ **Elevation Gain:** 10 m

🛒 **Stroller Friendly:** Yes

🚩 **GPS START:** 34.877421, 128.633293 (at the parking lot)

📍 **GPS POINT:** 34.884345, 128.628218 (at the road bridge)

🚩 **GPS FINISH:** 34.877421, 128.633293

HIKE DESCRIPTION

This area is very popular with families and young children for many reasons. In the summer there is a splashpad, and there is year-round bicycle riding for all ages on well-tended trails along a rather flat, small riverbank. This area of Geoje is one of only a few areas where young children can learn to ride a bike in relative safety. For the hike, after departing the parking lot, cross the bridge over the river. You will immediately find a large circular area covered in stone, which is always lively with kids and their scooters, bikes, and other toys. Off to your right is a small WC building and some outdoor picnic shelters, in addition to some outdoor gym equipment. You

will cross the circular plaza and turn left, heading up hill toward the splashpad. From the splashpad (which is extremely busy during the hot summer days), continue to the roller rink and stay along the riverbank roadway. Soon after the rink you will see an area suitable to venture out into the river to observe the various wildlife (like the white eastern great egret, the gray and/or purple heron, and several types of turtles). Kids will love to explore the slow waters of the Gohyeon River, which has small bands of fish hiding in the shadows of plants and snails, among other discoveries waiting to be found. Continuing on the trail, you will eventually come to a parking lot on your right and a bridge on your left. Cross the bridge and turn left for the river park trail along the banks of the river. Soon you will pass more outdoor gym equipment and many benches where you can take a rest. After another 800 meters, you will arrive back at the parking lot.

Hike 41 EASY

POW Camp Loop

⭐ **Rating:** Easy

〰️ **Route Type:** Loop

📍 **Distance:** 900 m

🕐 **Duration:** 2–3 hr (with numerous stops at exhibits)

⛰️ **Elevation Gain:** 25 m

🛒 **Stroller Friendly:** Yes (however, there are a few steps/stairs to negotiate)

🚩 **GPS START:** 34.875953, 128.625496 (at the parking lot entrance to the Fountain Square)

📍 **GPS POINT:** 34.876242, 128.623782 (at the barracks display)

🚩 **GPS FINISH:** 34.875953, 128.625496

HIKE DESCRIPTION

The Geoje Prisoner of War Camp experience, steeped in local and regional history, is touted as one of the premier sites in Geoje to visit. However, from a hiking perspective, this is a nice few hours spent on paved paths (with some stairs to negotiate in areas) as you encounter outdoor and indoor exhibitions about the Korean War (1950–1953) and the massive POW camp, which held over 170,000 POWs during the conflict. In the more modern part of the park (in Building 9), you can experience an immersive

sound and light show that simulates a town engulfed in combat with snipers all around, and a battlefield under machine gun staffing and artillery fire. It's not to be missed! Just near the end of the walk are many outdoor displays of heavy guns, helicopters, a jeep, and other relics of the wartime era.

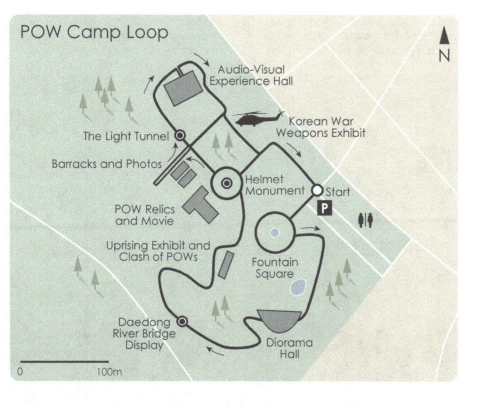

POW Camp Loop

- Audio-Visual Experience Hall
- Korean War Weapons Exhibit
- The Light Tunnel
- Barracks and Photos
- Helmet Monument
- Start
- POW Relics and Movie
- Uprising Exhibit and Clash of POWs
- Fountain Square
- Daedong River Bridge Display
- Diorama Hall

N

0   100m

Hike 42 EASY

Gohyeon/Suwol Two Valley Overlook Loop

⭐ **Rating:** Easy

↺ **Route Type:** Loop

📍 **Distance:** 3.5 km

🕐 **Duration:** 2–3 hr

🏔 **Elevation Gain:** 300 m

🚼 **Stroller Friendly:** No

🚩 **GPS START:** 34.877424, 128.633267 (at the parking lot)

🔺 **GPS SUMMIT:** 34.883037, 128.637838 (at the gazebo shelter)

🚩 **GPS FINISH:** 34.877424, 128.633267

HIKE DESCRIPTION

This hike offers amazing views over Gohyeon (Geoje City), Gyeryongsan, and the SHI shipyard. It starts at the parking lot adjacent to the children's park. Proceed across the bridge and bear to the left, passing the splashpad area and continuing to the roller rink. Pass the roller rink until you reach the northern corner, where you will see a small wooden bridge. Cross the bridge and turn right onto the dirt fire road

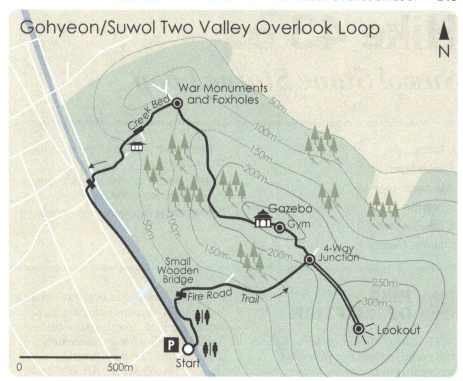

and head uphill. Follow the main path (it will bear to the right as it leaves the fire road) and avoid small trails going to graves and other places (there are a few of these). It will become quite steep until you reach the saddle atop the ridge.

At the ridgeline there is a bench and a four-way junction sign. (For those looking for a side trip, turn right heading to the southeast and hike approximately 800 meters to the highest point on the hill between Gohyeon and Suwol at 335 meters. Note that views are obstructed at this location by trees and brush.) After a rest, turn left and continue on the trail, enjoying the views over Gohyeon and Suwol Valleys through the trees. After 450 meters you will come to a clearing with some outdoor gym equipment, a rope swing, and a gazebo shelter, commanding unblocked views over Gohyeon and SHI from the rocky perch.

Continue on the trail past the gazebo and follow it steeply downhill along the undulating ridgeline in a northwesterly direction. After approximately 850 meters you will come to an area of old military earthworks (foxholes, etc.) and some graves a little farther on. Look for a small path on your left adjacent to these foxholes heading down along the edge of a rocky creek bed, and follow this path until you reach a small bridge, bearing to the left about 400 meters down the trail and departing the creek bed. After 100 meters, the trail skirts a small temple to the left and a fence to the right. Stay on the trail, and soon you will arrive at a road junction. Turn right and head down the hill, past the apartment buildings. You will pass a schoolyard on your right as you cross the bridge ahead of you. Once across the bridge, turn left and join the Gohyeon River trail. Follow it for another 900 meters until you arrive back at the parking lot.

Hike 43 `EASY`

Suwol Stone Statue Loop

⭐ **Rating:** Easy

↻ **Route Type:** Loop

📍 **Distance:** 4.6 km

🕐 **Duration:** 3 hr

⛰ **Elevation Gain:** 250 m

🛒 **Stroller Friendly:** No

🚩 **GPS START:** 34.893842, 128.645824 (at the parking area)

🔺 **GPS SUMMIT:** 34.898851, 128.651700 (at the stone statues at 307 m)

🏁 **GPS FINISH:** 34.893842, 128.645824

📖 HIKE DESCRIPTION

This loop hike offers lovely forest scenery with beautiful views from a smaller summit that has many stacked stones and stone statues surrounded by wildflowers in a clearing atop the ridgeline.

Start this hike from the apartment building up the hill and across the road from the sprawling Xii apartment complex in Suwol. Just opposite Building 106 you will see a dirt path running to nearby gardens. Take this path and begin heading uphill. After approximately 5 minutes you will reach a junction in the trail. If you go to the left, it will take you steeply to the summit, and if you go right, it will take you more gradually to the summit. On the trail map, I have shown only the gentler trail to the right. Continue on the trail until you reach the summit. **(Note: The summit will be just off**

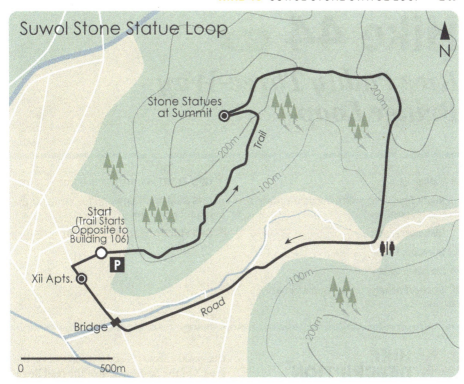

Suwol Stone Statue Loop

N

Stone Statues
at Summit

Trail

200m

100m

200m

Start
(Trail Starts
Opposite to
Building 106)

P

Xii Apts.

100m

Road

200m

Bridge

0   500m

to your left as you join the ridgeline trail about 25 meters away.)

Atop the summit, enjoy the stacked stones and the great views. If you hike in the summertime before the rice harvest, the rice paddies shimmer with brilliant shades of green to the northwest, while to the southeast the rocky nub of Little Guksabong stands proudly aloof, towering over the Suwol Valley like a prow of a ship. After admiring the views, backtrack to the junction (25 meters), and continue on the trail heading to the northeast along the ridgeline. Eventually the trail will bear to the right and head downhill, emerging alongside a creek bed in the valley. Opposite the road is a large WC and a trail map showing the trail that ascends toward Little Guksabong. However, for this hike you will cross the creek, join the paved roadway, and turn right, heading gently downhill. You will pass the WC, many private homes, and

kindergartens until you reach the main road junction as it crosses the small creek with a bridge and turns to the northwest. Continue on this road until you reach the church opposite the Xii apartments on your right-hand side, then turn right uphill and walk the final 200 meters to the parking lot of Building 106 where we began, completing the hike.

Hike 44 EASY

Rice Paddy Three-Way Bridge Loop

⭐ **Rating:** Easy

🔁 **Route Type:** Loop (with the option to extend at the midway point)

📍 **Distance:** 2.5 km

🕐 **Duration:** 1 hr

⛰ **Elevation Gain:** 3 m

🛻 **Stroller Friendly:** Yes (also great for bike riding!)

🚩 **GPS START:** 34.91137, 128.6531

🔺 **GPS SUMMIT:** 34.90383, 128.6460 (at the midpoint of the hike)

🚩 **GPS FINISH:** 34.91137, 128.6531

📖 HIKE DESCRIPTION

This hike starts from the road just behind the small police station located at the junction of Road 14 and Highway 1018 North. The hike takes you along newly constructed paved paths, which are also quite wide (3–4 meters). The area is very rare in Geoje, being both flat and not heavily built up with apartment or industrial buildings. There are multiple combinations of routes due to the many rice paddy access roads that crisscross the area. On the eastern side of the trail lies a shallow river (fed by the northern Geoje Reservoir 3.5 kilometers to the northeast and numerous natural creeks/streams from the surrounding hills) where fish, birds, turtles, and other wildlife can be seen. There are also many birds in the lush green rice paddies going about their hunting routines with little concern for passersby. The view of a slim-legged white egret hunting silently for tadpoles, crickets, etc. is typical on this hike.

At the approximate midway point of the hike, you may continue under the main road and along the river all the way to Gohyeon Harbor. This is a great extension of this loop hike (by adding an out-and-back route). The central feature among the lush green rice paddies of this area is a modern bridge that has three feeders, hence the name of this hike. If you wish to walk at night, this is also one of only a few locations where the bridge and trail paths along both sides of the river are lit along the entire length.

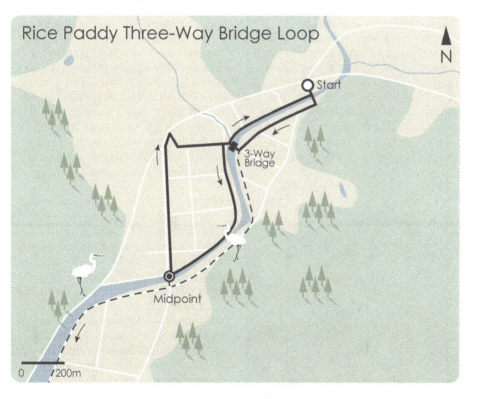

Rice Paddy Three-Way Bridge Loop

N

Start

3-Way
Bridge

Midpoint

0   200m

Hike 45 EASY

Chilcheon Island Footbridge Overlook Loop

⭐ **Rating:** Easy

🔄 **Route Type:** Loop

🧍‍♂️ **Distance:** 1.8 km

🕐 **Duration:** 1 hr

🏔 **Elevation Gain:** 75 m

🛒 **Stroller Friendly:** No (yes, from parking area to the bridge)

🚩 **GPS START:** 35.01302, 128.6408 (at the parking lot)

🔺 **GPS SUMMIT:** 35.01942, 128.6405 (at the gazebo)

🚩 **GPS FINISH:** 35.01302, 128.6408

 ## HIKE DESCRIPTION

Chilcheon Island is accessible by the Chilcheongyo Bridge on the northwest side of Geoje. This hike starts at the small fishing port where you can park your car. There are portable toilets here if you need them. Proceed along the harbor's edge, walking toward the footbridge. Cross the bridge and follow the trail until you reach the junction marker. Continue past the junction, staying on the main trail until you reach another junction (unmarked, but evident by the clear and wide trail heading straight up the hill). Head up the hill's switchbacks and steps until you reach the summit where the gazebo is located. The fantastic views will not disappoint! Once you have taken in the views (I have spent whole afternoons here) head back toward the bridge but go straight (do not take the trail you used to ascend the hill), and this will take you down a steep hill to the first junction marker. At the marker, turn left and head along the trail back to the bridge and parking area.

An optional addition to this loop hike is to continue from the gazebo down the hill in the opposite direction from the bridge. The trail goes steeply down and to the left and eventually meets up with the main trail you used to ascend. However, about halfway along the route, take a trail to the right (sometimes a bit overgrown but you will see it if you take care) and go approximately 100 meters farther. This will lead to a nice fenced-in platform with benches on the water's edge where you can fish or just relax.

Chilcheon Island Footbridge Overlook Loop

N

Water's Edge
Lookout

Gazebo
Lookout

Start

P

0   200m

Hike 46 `EASY`

Picnic Point Lookout

★ **Rating:** Easy

⌇ **Route Type:** Out and Back

📍 **Distance:** 500 m

🕐 **Duration:** 30–60 min

⛰ **Elevation Gain:** 30 m

🛒 **Stroller Friendly:** No

🚩 **GPS START:** 35.028888, 128.707887 (at the highway pull-off area adjacent to bus stop)

🔺 **GPS SUMMIT:** 35.029746, 128.709763 (at the gazebo)

🚩 **GPS FINISH:** 35.028888, 128.707887

 ## HIKE DESCRIPTION

This little hike can be accomplished by even the smallest of hikers! A short scramble from the roadside parking area leads through the forest to a winding path that heads up and around a hill to the top, where a small shelter offers views over the Geoje Grand Bridge toward Gadeok Island and the Busan New Port in the distance. There is always activity in the narrow body of water as fisherman, new-builds from SHI, and existing commercial and naval ships proceed to or from Jinhae (or Masan) Ports. A quick return by way of the same pathway back to the road completes this fun hike.

Hike 47 EASY

Daegeumsan Summit Loop

 Rating: Easy

Route Type: Loop

Distance: 3.6 km

Duration: 2–3 hr

Elevation Gain: 320 m

Stroller Friendly: No

GPS START: 34.956152, 128.691111 (at the parking lot)

GPS SUMMIT: 34.951662, 128.700011 (at Daegeumsan summit at 437.5 m)

GPS FINISH: 34.956152, 128.691111

HIKE DESCRIPTION

This is a very rewarding half-day hike to the summit of Daegeumsan, one of the "11 Famous Peaks of Geoje," which young children can also enjoy. There are only a few large steps in one section; otherwise, it is a well-worn path to the summit, offering spectacular views over the northern half of Geoje and to the mainland beyond.

The hike starts at the parking lot that has a large trail map and a WC. You'll see colorful hiking club ribbons near

the concrete fire road entrance, which is barred with a vehicular gate. Continue up the road, which starts off rather steep but will level out to a more comfortable slope after 300 meters. Don't be surprised to see black goats and other farm animals chewing on the underbrush, as there are many small farms in the vicinity. Continuing on the trail, you will see the summit of Daegeumsan standing far above you to the southeast as you clear the forest and approach a small, gated home on the right-hand side of the trail.

Continue past the gravel parking area (used in the spring Azalea Festival when thousands come to appreciate the colorful displays on the mountain's upper slopes) and a small pond on your right. The trail bears sharply to the right and then meets a junction with a marker where you will turn left and head uphill. This section of the trail is protected by mats that reduce wear and damage to the trail during its busier spring festival season.

Continuing on, you will reach a sunny meadow at the top of the trail and have the option to go either straight or turn right and go uphill through the numerous azalea bushes that enclose the trail like a

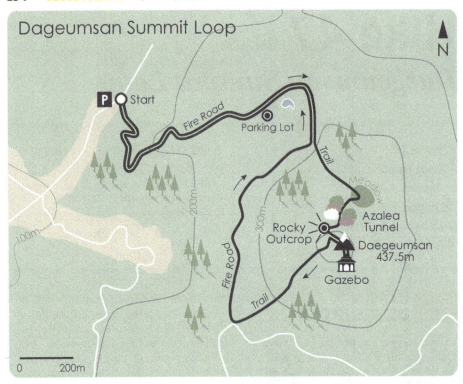

Dageumsan Summit Loop

tunnel. Turn right and head up the trail, through the tunnel. Near the top you will approach a large granite rock on the right that affords amazing views from the top, which is a mere scramble away. Having enjoyed the rocky outcrop, continue uphill, being careful on the steeper rock steps in the final 25 meters to the ridgeline. Once you reach the ridgeline, turn left and proceed toward the green fire watchtower, passing it on your right

as you reach the summit marker 20 meters beyond.

At 437.5 meters, the views are breathtaking from the summit. A bench sits adjacent to the summit marker where a rest can be taken; alternatively, just 25 meters farther on, there is a large gazebo shelter. After a rest, backtrack past the watchtower on your left and turn left onto the trail marked with numerous hiking club ribbons. Descend on this trail through the woods until you reach the fire road junction at the bottom. Turn right and follow the fire road until you emerge at the mat-covered trail. Just continue straight on the fire road, following the trail you used to approach the mountain all the way back to the parking lot.

Note: Hike 59 is the out-and-back version of this hike.

Hike 48 EASY

Pacific Codfish Trail

Rating: Easy

Route Type: Out and Back

Distance: 2.2 km

Duration: 2 hr

Elevation Gain: 225 m

Stroller Friendly: No

GPS START: 34.941524, 128.718744 (at the "Golden" Pacific Codfish Statue)

GPS SUMMIT: 34.946004, 128.723451 (at the northern observation platform at 226 m)

GPS FINISH: 34.941524, 128.718744

HIKE DESCRIPTION

This is a quick hike, and it's kid friendly—as long as they are good on stairs and steps! Start at the statue of the "Golden" Pacific Codfish. There is parking nearby in the small fishing port. Cross the bridge over the creek and bear to the right up the small concrete road toward the temple. Before you reach the temple, a staircase will come into view on your

left. Turn left and start the steep ascent up the many staircases to the ridgeline, making sure to stop along the way and enjoy the changing views as you quickly gain elevation.

At the ridgeline you have a choice to turn right or left. There are two observation platforms at each end of the two trails. One trail, about 150 meters to the left, leads to a platform at the high summit at 226 meters and the other, to the right about 300 meters, has a platform at about 190 meters in elevation. For this hike, you will turn left and head up to the high summit to enjoy the expansive observation platform and amazing views that span from Daegeumsan in the west, to the Geoje Grand Bridge in the north, and far out to sea to the east. Once you have enjoyed the peace and quiet, retrace your steps to the start point.

Hike 49 `EASY`

Deokpo Beach to Gangnamsan Smoke Tower Route

 Rating: Easy

Route Type: Out and Back

Distance: 2.4 km

Duration: 1 hr

Elevation Gain: 200 m

Stroller Friendly: No

GPS START: 34.911705, 128.710933 (at parking lot adjacent to the Penguins Statue)

GPS SUMMIT: 34.917802, 128.715138 (at smoke tower at 225 m)

GPS FINISH: 34.911705, 128.710933

HIKE DESCRIPTION

This is a great little hike for a morning refresh and recharge! Start by finding parking near the famous twin Penguin Statues at the beachfront of Deokpo Beach. Gazing out over the beach from the statue platform, head to your left toward the ridge of the hill looming up over the bay and town. Start by walking along the beach road until you reach the last main road on your left, then turn left and head uphill until you meet the main road. At the junction, turn right and stay on the sidewalk until you have just passed the motorway on/off ramp junction, and then cross the road, being careful of traffic. Once safely across the road, take the metal staircase up the escarpment. Follow the platform as you gain elevation. At the end of the metal platform, you'll find a proper trail as it quickly and steeply climbs the hillside toward the top. After hiking for a short time, you will emerge into a clearing and be rewarded with a lovely view of a rebuilt smoke-signal tower. Sitting on the stone tower and gazing out to sea,

it's not hard to feel like you are standing watch for hostile forces approaching from the sea. Such was the task 500 years ago when these towers were built. After enjoying the views and reading the historical marker, backtrack downhill to the beach. This completes the hike!

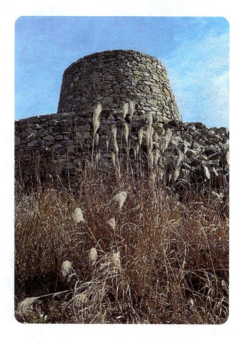

Deokpo Beach to Gangnamsan
Smoke Tower Route

N

Gangnamsan
Smoke Tower

200m

150m

100m

50m

Stairs

P

Start

Twin
Penguins

0   200m

Hike 50 EASY

Deokpo Beach to Okpo Great Victory Park Downhill Loop

⭐ **Rating:** Easy

🔄 **Route Type:** Loop

📍 **Distance:** 2.5 km

🕐 **Duration:** 1.5–2 hr (add at least 30–60 min if you want to explore the park as well)

⛰ **Elevation Gain:** 150 m

🛒 **Stroller Friendly:** No (yes, if you decide to hike out and back via the paved road only)

🚩 **GPS START:** 34.911664, 128.710958

📍 **GPS POINT:** 34.900735, 128.713882 (at the Okpo Great Victory Park Visitor Center)

🚩 **GPS FINISH:** 34.911664, 128.710958

📖 HIKE DESCRIPTION

After finding parking on a side street or bare ground one or two blocks in from the beach, proceed on foot to the seafront and make your way to the "Twin Penguins" statue. From this location, a beautiful view of Deokpo Beach spreads out before you from the northeast to the southwest. Looking straight out from the beach, Deokpo Bay is always alive with fishing activity and ship traffic entering and departing Okpo Bay past the breakwaters. For this hike, start by moving along the beach road to the southwest and then head inland toward the red metal bridge. At the entrance to the bridge, you will not cross but instead continue along the top of the concrete pathway that lines the stream and heads to the main road. You will pass garden plots on the right with views of the small golf course on the far side of the stream nestled below the hill. At the road junction, turn left, cross the bridge, and stay on the sidewalk while heading up the hill, passing the coffee shop on the right and the golf course on the left. After you reach the top of the hill, cross the road at the junction and turn left, heading downhill past private homes, pensions, and restaurants on your right. The boardwalk allows you to stay off the winding roadway and enjoy the lovely views through the trees toward Okpo Bay and the DSME Shipyard. You might see various floating docks and outfitting piers while a flotilla of barges and tugs scurry about with material needed for ship construction. Looming across the bay is the majestic Okneyobong, standing tall at 554.7 meters. Continuing down the road for a few more minutes, you will reach the Okpo Great Victory Commemorative Park.

Following the payment of a modest fee at the tollbooth, continue across the parking lot into the two-story visitor center and museum. **(Note: There is drinking water and a WC available on the ground floor just inside the entrance to the right.)** The museum displays and

玉浦大捷紀念塔

Deokpo Beach to Okpo Great Victory Park
Downhill Loop

N

Start Deokpo
Beach

Twin
Penguins

Concrete Road

Red
Steel
Bridge

Deokpo Bay

Rock Pools and
Pebble Beach

Wood
Bridge

100m

100m

Monument

Gym Pavillion

Shrine Museum

Toll

Okpo Bay Overlook

0   200m

models really bring local history to life and explain why Korea and Japan have had a rather troubled relationship for more than 500 years. After departing the museum, head over to the scale models of the famous Korean "Turtle Ships" and then proceed up the steps to the shrine for Admiral Yi Sun-sin—the famous Choson-era admiral who defeated the Japanese in a series of famous sea battles nearby. From the shrine, continue along the marked path and up the paved road to the Okporu Pavilion and 30-meter-high Battles and Victory Monument. Enjoy the large, covered pavilion and the views of Deokpo Bay, as well as a cooling sea breeze.

Once your visit to the park is complete, retrace your steps out of the park and continue back up the road past the overlook point until you reach a crossing with a set of steps heading downhill and another set of steps heading uphill across the road. At this juncture, cross the road and head up the steps onto the forest path. After a few minutes, some gym equipment will come into view. Just stay on the trail and enjoy the view along the undulating coastal track back to the red metal bridge at Deokpo Beach. As a short side trip, about halfway along the track at a low point adjacent to a small creek crossing, you will notice a small wooden bridge on your right-hand side. Depart the main trail and turn right, crossing the bridge. Carry on for 5 minutes down to the rocky beachfront along Deokpo Bay. At this location you can do some fishing from the rocks or simply enjoy the sound of the waves lapping along the stones. There are also tidal rock pools to explore in this area. Back on the main trail, after the red metal bridge, it's only a 2-minute walk back to the starting point at the Penguins Statue and a well-deserved rest along the beachfront.

Hike 51 EASY

Okpo International Park

⭐ **Rating:** Easy

🔄 **Route Type:** Loop (option for out and back to overlook via hilltop gazebo)

📏 **Distance:** 0.7 km

🕐 **Duration:** 1 hr

⛰ **Elevation Gain:** 25 m

🛒 **Stroller Friendly:** Yes (but the hilltop gazebo has a few steps on both sides that must be carefully negotiated)

🚩 **GPS START:** 34.893876, 128.703057 (at the parking lot)

🔺 **GPS SUMMIT:** 34.896919, 128.703234 (at the lookout point)

🚩 **GPS FINISH:** 34.893876, 128.703057

HIKE DESCRIPTION

Okpo International Park has many options, especially for families with younger children. There are two gazebo shelters, one near the playground and WC and another atop a hill overlooking the park. Both make for nice places to people-watch and have a picnic. The playground is for children under 10 years of age, but there is also an outdoor gym for adults adjacent to the playground. If you want to teach your children to ride a bike, this is the best place on Geoje. The paved bike path encircles the park and has plenty of shade from a selection of local trees. In the springtime there are many cherry blossom trees here as well. For a truly awe-inspiring view over Okpo Bay and the DSME Shipyard, just walk past the hilltop gazebo and follow the sidewalk to the lookout point approximately 200 meters past the gazebo.

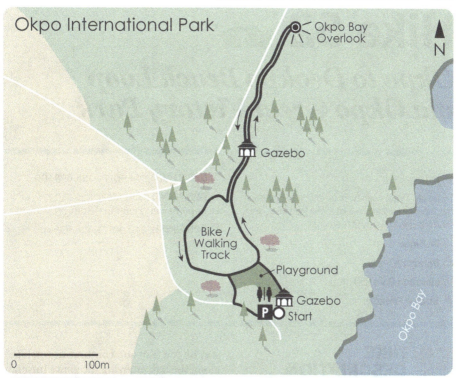

Okpo International Park

Okpo Bay Overlook

N

Gazebo

Bike / Walking Track

Playground

Gazebo

Start

Okpo Bay

0   100m

Hike 52 EASY

Okpo to Deokpo Beach Loop via Okpo Great Victory Park

⭐ **Rating:** Easy

🔄 **Route Type:** Loop (with an option to bypass at the midway point and return to the beginning, thus shortening the hike by 50 percent)

📏 **Distance:** 6 km

🕐 **Duration:** 3–5 hr

⛰️ **Elevation Gain:** 150 m

🛒 **Stroller Friendly:** No

🚩 **GPS START:** 34.890174, 128.699400

📍 **GPS POINT:** 34.9116534,128.710976 (at Deokpo Beach "Penguins" Statue)

🚩 **GPS FINISH:** 34.890174, 128.699400

📖 HIKE DESCRIPTION

This particular hike is fantastic in any weather and for any experience level. Start off on the far side of the Okpo Fishing Harbor basin, which is teeming with activity. Its perimeter is lined with colorful restaurants and pubs, which offer a multitude of fresh seafood to enjoy. Moving beyond the activity of the port, on the bay side there is a wooden platform and trail map, which is the beginning of the hike. For the first several hundred meters, the trail is wood-composite boardwalk that hugs the rocky coastline and offers amazing views of the harbor and the DSME Shipyard. Sightings of fish and all sorts of small sea creatures are commonplace on this stretch of the trail.

After a few minutes, the boardwalk ends and a rather steep, albeit short, stretch of proper forested trail begins before it offers a choice—to go downward on the trail or upward toward the Okpo International Park (see Hike 51). For this hike,

stay on the trail and continue downslope along the bay, enjoying the views through the forest and out to sea. After about 30 minutes, a small village will come into sight, full of colorful roofs and pensions available to rent, interspersed with a few restaurants. The trail continues right along the seafront, passing a nice shingle beach (a great place to skip stones with the kids), and bears right along the harbor front on a concrete seawall road to the end, where the trail continues up a metal staircase. Many anglers enjoy this particular spot on the bay, and you will rarely be alone on this part of the trail.

Continuing up the stairs, you will pass some vegetable plots and soon come to wooden stairs and a road crossing. At this juncture, cross the road and take the steps up into the forest to continue your trek. (There are options here for a short, 2-minute side trip downhill to the right that leads to a lovely Okpo Bay overlook before crossing the road and continuing on. Alternatively, this is a great place to cut the hike in half and head uphill to the

Okpo to Deokpo Beach Loop via Okpo Great Victory Park

left until you reach the main road and then take another left back to Okpo.)

After a few minutes, you will reach an outdoor gym and continue on the trail. The next part of the trail is among the more wild and enjoyable sections, with cliffside panoramas with crashing waves far below, large aquaculture buoy spreads at the entrance of Deokpo Bay, and fishermen attending to their nets. Farther up the trail, a deep grove of cedar trees lines a steep section of trail that hides a small creek trickling down to the bay.

All along the length of the trail are historical markers about Japanese-Korean sea battles, including a famous maritime battle that took place here during the Japanese invasion of 1592–1597, in which Korean admiral Yi Sun-sin defeated the invading Japanese fleet despite being heavily outnumbered.

Continuing on the trail, you will soon have Deokpo Beach clearly in sight, and after few steep steps down you will cross a red metal bridge over a small creek. Taking a sharp right at the end of the bridge leads you to the beachfront and the famous Deokpo "Penguins" statue. Each January, the famous Penguin Swimming Festival is held here, during which hundreds of participants race into the chilly waters for a swim—with plenty of admiration and hot tea afterwards!

Deokpo Beach is the natural midway point on this hike and a great place to take a rest. Near the beach, enjoy a snack and a drink. Public restrooms are also available at the far end of the beach or in nearby coffeehouses.

After you have enjoyed your rest, backtrack to the red metal bridge, but this time do not cross it. Instead, follow the concrete path along the creek all the way to the main road and then turn left, crossing the bridge and heading up the hill. Across the street there is both a coffee shop and a convenience store. This stretch of the hike is all paved sidewalk heading back to Okpo, and the next 15 minutes is lacking in scenery. However, this will change once you crest the hilltop and start along the ridge overlooking Okpo Bay. Depending on the season, this stretch of the hike is full of amazing vantage points over the coastline and many amazing wildflowers. As you pass the Okpo Bay overlook (see Hike 51), you will continue down the hill, staying on the sidewalk until you are about 300 meters from the main intersection where a supermarket is located. At this point, take the road off to the left, making your first right down the hill, and continue straight past the playground at the bottom of the hill on your right. Just 5 minutes ahead lies Okpo Fishing Harbor where you began your hike.

Hike 53 EASY

Battleship Park and Okpo Waterfront

⭐ **Rating:** Easy

🔄 **Route Type:** Loop

📍 **Distance:** 1.5 km

🕐 **Duration:** 1–2 hr

🏔 **Elevation Gain:** None

🛒 **Stroller Friendly:** Yes

🚩 **GPS START:** 34.888088, 128.694620 (at the Turtle Ship replica)

🔺 **GPS SUMMIT:** 34.890587, 128.696352 (at corner of the fishing boat park across the street from the Geoje Ocean Hotel)

🚩 **GPS FINISH:** 34.888088, 128.694620

 ## HIKE DESCRIPTION

This is a lovely stroll that takes in 500 years of Okpo history in a short loop hike along the waterfront of the city. Begin at the full-size replica of a Joseon-era wooden warship referred to as a "Turtle Ship," which was used by the famous Korean admiral Yi Sun-sin to defeat the Japanese in a series of maritime battles during the Japanese Invasions (Imjin War) of 1592–1598. The replica is placed ashore in the harborside park opposite

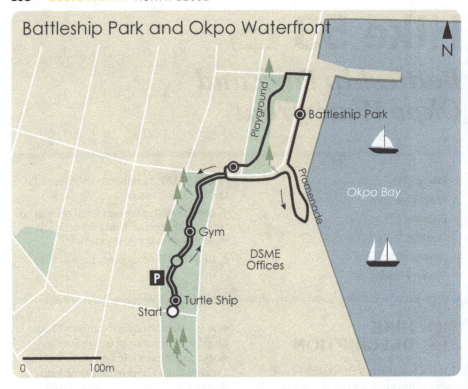

Battleship Park and Okpo Waterfront

N

Playground

Battleship Park

Promenade

Okpo Bay

Gym

DSME
Offices

P

Turtle Ship

Start

0   100m

the DSME office buildings and is open to the public. The ship contains many displays of interest and offers visitors the opportunity to try rowing an oar or moving the tiller. (The ship is wheelchair and stroller accessible with a ramp leading up to allow access onboard.)

Proceed from the ship through the park, heading north until the park ends, then turn right toward the harbor, passing along the DSME office building and bearing to your right onto a lovely waterfront promenade. This area is fully enclosed and offers some shade and a series of benches where you can relax. If you have kids, they can run around safely here. From here, the modern skills of Korean shipbuilders are clearly in view at the enormous DSME Shipyard.

Continuing on, head north from the promenade to a newly constructed waterfront park that stretches into Okpo

Bay and lies just adjacent to the opening of the old Okpo Fishing Harbor (still bustling with activity and well worth a visit!). Having enjoyed the waterfront, now cross the street adjacent to the Geoje Ocean Hotel and start your walk south back toward the Turtle Ship, stopping at the playground and perhaps midway at the convenience store. One great aspect of most convenience stores in Korea is that they have ample space outdoors to relax, snack, and people-watch. Continuing south, you will soon arrive back at the Turtle Ship, completing this hike.

Note: Ample parking can be found adjacent to the small harbor front park.

Hike 54 `EASY`

Yangjiam Lighthouse via Neungpo-dong Sculpture Park Loop

Rating: Easy

Route Type: Loop

Distance: 5 km

Duration: 3–4 hr

Elevation Gain: 150 m

Stroller Friendly: No (Yes, if modifications are made to the route. See the note at the end of the hike description.)

GPS START: 34.877047, 128.737430 (at the Sculpture Park parking lot)

GPS POINT: 34.895325, 128.751521 (at Yangjiam Lighthouse)

GPS FINISH: 34.877047, 128.737430

HIKE DESCRIPTION

This hike has elements of everything beautiful about Geoje: amazing seascapes, views of ships at anchor, locals growing vegetables (including the ever-present Korean red chilies), and fantastic gazebo rest areas. There are also views of crashing waves on rocky cliffs far below, and on clear days, views of the entire northeast coast of the island, including the distant but visible Geoje Grand Bridge and the tower blocks of Pusan's westernmost suburbs.

Start this hike at the small parking lot (a WC is available on the eastern side of the lot) at the western side and follow the well-marked trail as it makes its way downhill after 75 meters. Halfway along this trail you will find a playground. A bit farther along the trail, you will see many sculptures in a manicured park setting (with two more WCs). After enjoying

the sculptures, continue on the trail as it rises and falls along the pine-scented peninsula, which rapidly narrows. Soon you will pass a gazebo shelter on your right, a second playground, and an outdoor gym on your left at the bottom of the hill. From here you can enjoy beautiful views to the north-northwest.

Continue on the trail, and soon you will come to a trail map and dirt path into the woods on your right-hand side. Venture into the woods, bearing to the left at first and continuing uphill. (There are other trails leading down to the rocky coast that are frequented by fishermen.) After a few minutes the path will become steeper, broken only by one rest spot with a raised wooden platform and a very popular hammock.

Continue on the trail and make the final steep ascent to the high point where a gazebo shelter and rest spot are located. The views out to sea are fabulous at this

Yangjiam Lighthouse via Neungpo-dong Sculpture Park Loop

N

Yangjiam Lighthouse

Stairs and Bridge

Gazebo

Playground

Gazebo

East Sea

Sculptures

Start P

0   500m

location and the sea breeze will make you feel happy to be alive! After enjoying this special spot, continue on the trail as it undulates down and up the narrowing peninsula (with water views through the trees on both sides). After a final push up a steep hill (the trail is quite close to the edge of the cliff), the trail bears to the left and goes steeply downhill to merge with a small roadway that runs the length of the peninsula.

Stepping onto the road, turn right and continue to the very end, passing the vehicular gate, which may or may not be open. After this gate, the road goes uphill for a few minutes until you come to a gate you cannot pass. On the other side of this gate you will see (and hear) a facility that trains police dogs. Just before the gate there is a small signpost and a path leading downhill to the left. Take the path downhill and cross the small wooden bridge over a gully, then

follow the path along the outer edge of the fence until it broadens into a dirt road. Be careful to stay on the main trail and bear to the left heading downhill. After a minute you will see your first good view of the sparkling white Yangjiam Lighthouse high above you on a rocky outcrop—a sentinel against the ravages of the mighty sea! Continuing on the trail, you will pass a high set of red metal steps until reaching the lighthouse proper, but continue past the lighthouse and make your way the final 30 meters or so to the very end of the trail, which at this point consists of metal and wood planks bound to the high rocky cliffs and surrounded by wire and wood fencing.

At the terminus, you can enjoy views out to sea and along the coastline of rugged Geoje as the waves crash far below and the sea birds wheel overhead. This is a very special place! Once the time has come to rest, take a break from the wind in and around the lighthouse proper.

When you're ready, make your way all the way back to the small road near the gate. Stay on the road and take it all the way back (approximately 1 kilometer) until you hit the junction of another road on your left, closed with a vehicular gate that's easy to climb over or go around on foot. Take this road to the left, pass the bar gate, and walk for a few minutes until you find yourself back at the trail map (now on your left). Continue on the main path (not into the forest!), passing the playground and the gazebo rest area. Continue past the sculptures and soon

you will be at the parking lot where the hike began.

Note: This hike can be made to suit those with a stroller by simply avoiding the forest trail. Departing the playground, continue past the path entrance (with the trail sign on the right) and stay straight on the trail until you reach the vehicular gate, turning right onto the concrete road at the junction and going all the way to the end just before the police dog gatehouse. At that point you would need to cable lock your stroller, or just leave it at the top of the trail, before you make the final push on foot to the lighthouse.

Hike 55 `EASY`

Camelia (Jisimdo) Island Loop Route

- ⭐ **Rating:** Easy
- **Route Type:** Loop
- **Distance:** 3.8 km
- 🕐 **Duration:** 3–4 hr (with stops included)
- **Elevation Gain:** 50 m
- **Stroller Friendly:** Yes (but there are a few steps near the northern and southern overlooks)

🚩 **GPS START:** 34.867175, 128.727562 (at Jangseungpo Camelia Island Ferry Terminal)

📍 **GPS POINT:** 34.817508, 128.747590 (at Camelia Island Ferry Terminal)

📍 **GPS POINT:** 34.826294, 128.754575 (at Northern Overlook)

📍 **GPS POINT:** 34.814883, 128.746158 (at Southern Overlook)

🚩 **GPS FINISH:** 34.867175, 128.727562

📖 HIKE DESCRIPTION

The only way to access Camelia Island (Jisimdo) is by passenger ferry from Geoje. Camelia Island is famous for its lovely red flowers of the same name and also for the fact that it is a vehicle-free zone. The trails are wide and easy to navigate, and people of all ages and abilities can enjoy hiking there.

The crossing from Jangseungpo Harbor lasts only 20 minutes. Once you have arrived at the small ferry terminal on the island, a short concrete path leads up to a small settlement with a dozen or so houses and several restaurants with outdoor terraces that have amazing views westward toward Geoje.

Proceeding in a northerly direction from the village, the main pathway leads along the length of the island for about 1 kilometer until you reach a

junction where the east coast path turns southwards, or you can take the northern overlook route the final 300 meters to the end of the island to enjoy the views from

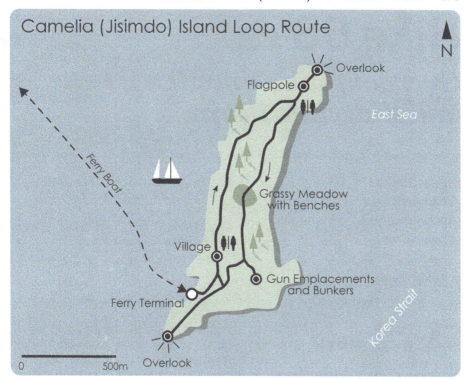

Camelia (Jisimdo) Island Loop Route

atop the rocky cliffs. Along the way you will come across a flagpole mast, which was used by the Japanese military in the colonial era while they were in possession of the island, but which now proudly flies the Korean flag. Farther on, before the final overlook, is a little alcove on your right-hand side with a secluded bench for two and peaceful views out to sea.

Backtracking from the overlook point, make your way back to the junction and turn to the left, following the trail headed in a southerly direction as it passes through the forest and cultivated plots with vegetables, until you reach a grassy cleared field with sculptures and benches. From this vantage point, views to the east and west abound, and a set of mounted binoculars offers views out to sea toward the east. Continue on the trail to the south and you will soon hit another junction that offers a side trip down to the Japanese 1930s-era shore

gun emplacements and ammunition bunkers on the left. Take the trail down the hill and read the detailed historical markers while exploring the rather dim and moldy-smelling bunkers.

Retrace your steps back uphill to the junction and follow the path as it leads past the lighthouse and around the periphery of the power plant and heads toward the southern tip of the island, with its rocky finger pointed into the sea. Near the end, be careful on the rocky cliffs. A nice bench is affixed near the end point, where you can enjoy views to the north of the island.

Head back toward the village area following the well-marked trail and descend back down toward the ferry terminal, which offers a circular rest house with generous seating. A quick and pleasant ride on the ferry will take you back to Jangseungpo Harbor.

Hike 56 `MODERATE`

Gyeryongsan Summit and Ridgeline Loop

- ⭐ **Rating:** Moderate
- 🔁 **Route Type:** Loop
- 🐾 **Distance:** 6.6 km
- 🕐 **Duration:** 4 hr
- 📈 **Elevation Gain:** 500 m
- 🛒 **Stroller Friendly:** No

🚩 **GPS START:** 34.883197, 128.612546 (along the road near the high school and stadium)

🔺 **GPS SUMMIT:** 34.870367, 128.608234 (at Gyeryongsan summit at 566 m)

🚩 **GPS FINISH:** 34.883197, 128.612546

HIKE DESCRIPTION

This hike is a favorite in the Gohyeon Valley among locals and foreigners alike. Many (predominantly foreign) residential apartment complexes are perched on the southwestern slopes of this mountain, offering numerous trails that link to the summit ridgeline trail.

Begin by parking along the roadway just past the Gohyeon Stadium and high school, making your way from the trail

sign past several community gardens until you reach the base of a white steel footbridge that crosses the highway. Once past the highway, continue on the trail as it passes into deep forest. Head uphill about 500 meters until you emerge onto a fire road. Cross the fire road to the trail opposite. Get ready for the next 500 meters to the ridgeline, which is very steep and unrelenting!

At the top of the trail, you will emerge next to a gazebo shelter and observation deck, which offers fabulous views. After

Gyeryongsan Summit and Ridgeline Loop

N

Overlook

Bench

300m

Rocky Trail

Fire Road

400m

200m

100m

P

Start

Stadium

500m

Gazebo

Gyeryongsan
566m

0   500m

you have caught your breath, continue past the gazebo and bear to the left heading southward toward the summit (there is another trail heading off to the right and northwest, but do not take this trail). You will travel over a few rocky outcrops, down a steel staircase, under a high-voltage power pylon, and soon arrive at the base of a large rock where you will see the summit marker. Be careful not to pass the stone marker, as just beyond it, there is a dropoff from a minor cliff.

Sitting atop the summit of the second-highest mountain on Geoje, you can admire most of the peaks across Geoje and enjoy amazing views across the Gohyeon and Suwol Valleys to Little (and Big) Guksabong. After you have taken in the grandeur, climb down and backtrack to the gazebo shelter. Just as you approach the shelter, take the trail on your left and head downhill northwest-

ward along the rocky ridgeline. In some places you will find yourself squeezing around and over a few rocky outcrops, but the trail remains clear all the way. The ridge slowly drops in elevation, and off to your left just beyond the trees is a golf course and apartment buildings. The trail ends amidst some benches and gym equipment and joins a concrete fire road. Turn right and follow the road for about 500 meters until you meet the junction of a gravel fire road.

Across the road is an observation platform with a magnificent overlook at an elevation of 240 meters. From the overlook, continue on the gravel fire road heading to the south-southeast until you reach the trail crossing where you first crossed the road on your uphill segment. Turn left and go downhill to the steel footbridge, cross the highway, and return to the parking location on the road where you began the hike.

Hike 57 `MODERATE`

Gyeryongsan Summit via Geoje City Hall Loop

- ★ **Rating:** Moderate
- **Route Type:** Loop
- **Distance:** 5.2 km
- **Duration:** 4–5 hr
- **Elevation Gain:** 500 m
- **Stroller Friendly:** No

🚩 **GPS START:** 34.883197, 128.612546 (same as Hike 56)

🔺 **GPS SUMMIT:** 34.870367, 128.608234 (at Gyeryongsan summit at 566 m)

🚩 **GPS FINISH:** 34.883197, 128.612546

HIKE DESCRIPTION

This hike offers vast panoramas and a visit to the small but charming temple of Gyelyongsa. It begins at the same location as Hike 56 and follows the same route and waypoints all the way up to the summit marker at 566 meters. However, from the summit, you will then proceed to the southeast, following the rocky ridgeline and cutting in and out

Gyeryongsan Summit via Geoje City Hall Loop

of scrubby brush until you emerge at a concrete blockhouse and a steel pylon/antenna. From this location, follow the concrete road downhill until it opens up to a large observation platform adjacent to the monorail transport. You can either take the monorail back down to the valley or keep on hiking!

Continuing on, the trail follows along the monorail tracks and rapidly loses elevation, crossing the fire road and then bearing northward for the final 400 meters. The trail emerges from the forest adjacent to the temple. Once you have visited the temple, continue past the café and follow the narrow paved road down to the main road. At the intersection, turn left and proceed past the city hall (see Hike 39) until you reach the stadium road. Again, turn left and pass the stadium as you proceed back up the access road to the parking lot where you began the hike.

Hike 58 MODERATE

Aengsan Summit Route

⭐ **Rating:** Moderate

🔄 **Route Type:** Out and Back

📏 **Distance:** 5 km

🕐 **Duration:** 3 hr

⛰️ **Elevation Gain:** 450 m

🛒 **Stroller Friendly:** No

🚩 **GPS START:** 34.944825, 128.630395 (at the Yugye Village reservoir parking location)

🔺 **GPS SUMMIT:** 34.940636, 128.614003 (at Aengsan summit at 507.4 m)

🚩 **GPS FINISH:** 34.944825, 128.630395

HIKE DESCRIPTION

Aengsan towers over Gohyeon Bay and SHI. In the winter, the upper 50 meters of this peak will be so coated in ice that it will glow when the sun hits it. The hike begins at the reservoir above Yugye village, where there is room for a few cars along the edge of the reservoir. From the parking site, proceed on foot following the road for 1.5 kilometers, passing the lovely Gwangcheongsa Temple on your left. Soon the road comes to a roundabout, and the footpath continues steeply uphill from here. After about

500 meters there is a small rest area with some benches before the final 500 meters uphill to the summit marker. The views from the summit are spectacular, especially over SHI and Gohyeon City. A large gazebo shelter stands 50 meters from the summit and makes for a lovely spot for a rest. Backtrack along the route to complete the hike.

Note: If you want to make this a shorter version of the same hike, drive to the roundabout and hike the 1 kilometer to the summit in 1 hour. The trail map shows both routes for clarity.

Aengsan Summit Route

N

Reservoir
Start

Gwangcheongsa
Temple

Aengsan
507.4m

Roundabout
Start

0   500m

Hike 59 MODERATE

Daegeumsan Summit Route

- ⭐ **Rating:** Moderate
- 🔄 **Route Type:** Out and Back
- 📍 **Distance:** 4 km
- 🕐 **Duration:** 2–3 hr
- ⛰ **Elevation Gain:** 320 m
- 🚼 **Stroller Friendly:** No

- 🚩 **GPS START:** 34.956152, 128.691111 (at the parking lot)
- 🔺 **GPS SUMMIT:** 34.951662, 128.700011 (at Daegeumsan summit at 437.5 m)
- 🚩 **GPS FINISH:** 34.956152, 128.691111

📖 HIKE DESCRIPTION

Daegeumsan is one of those great little peaks that offers year-round hiking for all classes of hikers, with something a little different to enjoy in each season.

This hike was previously described in detail (see Hike 47). The key difference between Hike 47 and 59 is that you will return along the same route you used to make the summit.

Note: Some hikers may have trouble finding the trail again. It is advisable to hang marker tape on a branch when you are on your way up to avoid missing the turn on your way back down.

Daegeumsan Summit Route

Hike 60 MODERATE

Guksabong (and Little Guksabong) Summit Route

⭐ **Rating:** Moderate

🔄 **Route Type:** Out and Back

📍 **Distance:** 5.2 km

🕐 **Duration:** 3 hr

🏔 **Elevation Gain:** 475 m

🛒 **Stroller Friendly:** No

🚩 **GPS START:** 34.890058, 128.686095 (at 200 m behind the Admiral Hotel, to the right and uphill)

🔺 **GPS SUMMIT:** 34.884822, 128.672168 (at Guksabong summit at 464 m)

🔺 **GPS SUMMIT:** 34.886042, 128.665105 (at Little Guksabong summit at 387 m)

🚩 **GPS FINISH:** 34.890058, 128.686095

HIKE DESCRIPTION

This hike is perhaps one of the most popular and well-worn trails on all of Geoje. This was the first trail I hiked in Korea in 1995, when I was first posted to Geoje. Despite its popularity, you should still be able to enjoy peace and quiet for the most part.

This hike starts in Okpo just 200 meters behind the old Okpo Daewoo Tourist Hotel (renamed the Admiral Hotel), at a concrete road that has an open gate and green sign with the name of the mountain in both Hangul and English. Follow the concrete road as it twists uphill, passing a boot-cleaning station on your left. Atop the hill, as the road transitions to gravel, you will see a series of stone steps on your right-hand side leading to a path. Take the steps and proceed on the path, which will pass over a small bridge, behind a small temple building, and into the forest. After passing another creek (this area is frequented by small "water deer" so don't be surprised if you see one or hear one rustling in the bushes!) a series of stone steps rises ahead, and the path climbs steeply uphill with a series of switchbacks until you reach the ridgeline.

At the ridgeline there is a trail junction with exercise equipment and, more importantly, a bench. I recommend taking a brief rest before beginning the steep ascent! For this hike, you will turn left toward the summit and follow the ridgeline, with a gradual increase in elevation and lovely views through the trees on both sides of the trail. Soon the trail will open up to a clearing with more

exercise machines and a shelter with viewing platform on your left. The view from this platform is spectacular—all of Okpo lies below you in clear view.

Depart the shelter area and be careful as you approach the main junction as the trail splits to the right and left. Make sure to bear to the right and follow this trail as it passes a clearing and begins to climb uphill again, getting steeper as you approach the summit. The views are constrained by heavy foliage until you break out of the forest, and a large rocky outcrop with a bench appears.

This is the first of two amazing views from the summit area. From this rock you can enjoy an uninterrupted view of the Aju-dong Valley, Okneyobong, all of DSME, Okpo Bay, and Okpo. After enjoying the spectacular views, proceed to the nearby gazebo shelter and pass under it, staying on the trail for another

25 meters until you see the summit marker.

Here you can enjoy expansive views to the south, including Suwol and SHI beyond, despite some low bushes. From the summit marker, backtrack 10 meters to the trail and turn left toward Little Guksabong, a rocky nub about 400 meters from Guksabong proper.

The trail descends steeply, and a rope/chain adjacent to the trail provides handholds as you descend to the ridgeline saddle before encountering a staircase that takes you to the rocky open summit of Little Guksabong. From this favored outcrop, the view over Suwol to Gohyeon and SHI is unsurpassed.

Backtrack on the route, with care taken at the main junction points to ensure you do not take one of the many other trails leading back down to Okpo.

Hike 61 MODERATE

Guksabong Summit Loop Route via ISK School

⭐ **Rating:** Moderate

〰️ **Route Type:** Loop

📍 **Distance:** 4.5 km

🕐 **Duration:** 2.5 hr

⛰️ **Elevation Gain:** 425 m

🛒 **Stroller Friendly:** No

🚩 **GPS START:** 34.890151, 128.688327 (at the Admiral Hotel)

🔺 **GPS SUMMIT:** 34.884822, 128.672168 (at Guksabong summit at 464 m)

📍 **GPS POINT:** 34.888394, 128.689858 (at ISK School)

🚩 **GPS FINISH:** 34.890151, 128.688327 (at the Admiral Hotel)

HIKE DESCRIPTION

This hike begins in front of the Admiral Hotel. From the hotel, skirt around the outside to the north and bear right at the road junction behind the hotel, going uphill for about 100 meters until you see an opening in the chain-link fence and the green sign for Guksabong.

Guksabong Summit Loop Route via ISK School

N

200m

Stone Steps

Stone Steps

Trail Marker

P

Start

Parking Lot

Admiral Hotel

LotteMart

Elcru

ISK School

3-Way Junction

Steep

300m

100m

Guksabong 464m

Gazebo

400m

Lookout Point

Viewpoint Toward Summit

300m

200m

Gym

4-Way Junction
Sign for Daewoo Apt.

0   500m

Follow the trail notes from Hike 60 until you reach the summit of Guksabong.

From the summit, backtrack down the mountain to the clearing with the gym equipment and overlook. Bear right following the trail to the southeast until you come to a four-way junction with some gym equipment and a marker that reads "Daewoo Apt." Take this trail to the left, heading downhill. After about 800 meters, a clearing will allow for a nice view back toward the rock-encrusted summit of Guksabong. After a short distance, you will emerge from the trees and bear to the left downhill on the road. Follow it as it doglegs right past ISK (International School of Koje) until you hit the four-way road junction at the bottom of the hill. A short 200-meter walk to the left and then right will take you back to the Admiral Hotel. **(Note: Do expect to run into wildlife during night hikes here and elsewhere on Geoje. If you see glowing eyes in the dark, it is usually just small "water deer.")**

Hike 62 MODERATE

Guksabong Summit Loop via Aju-dong and DSME

⭐ **Rating:** Moderate

🔁 **Route Type:** Loop

📍 **Distance:** 7.2 km

🕐 **Duration:** 4 hr

⛰️ **Elevation Gain:** 425 m

🛒 **Stroller Friendly:** No

🚩 **GPS START:** 34.890151, 128.688327 (at the Admiral Hotel)

🔺 **GPS SUMMIT:** 34.884822, 128.672168 (at Guksabong summit at 464 m)

🏁 **GPS FINISH:** 34.890151, 128.688327

HIKE DESCRIPTION

Refer to Hike 61 and follow the directions until you reach the four-way junction with the "Daewoo Apartments" sign. At this point do not turn left or right, but stay on the trail, going straight. The trail will pass through some lovely forest and will undulate up and down a bit as you head downslope to the southeast in the direction of Aju-dong. Soon you will hear the sounds of DSME Shipyard, and the large yellow gantry crane will come into view, as will the towers of the Everville Apartment Complex. Follow the trail as it approaches the Everville complex and follow it downhill through some ad hoc gardens, bearing to the left until the trail abruptly ends in a parking area.

Walk straight for about 25 meters and then turn right onto a small road, passing a supermarket on your left, until you reach the main road opposite DSME Shipyard. At the main road, turn left and walk to the first set of lights at the four-way road junction. Cross the road here heading toward DSME and follow the road as it skirts the shipyard toward downtown Okpo.

Marvel at close-up views of some of the world's largest container ships. Soon you will pass the life-size replica of a fifteenth-century Korean Turtle Ship (see Hike 53). Continue on for about 85 meters to the three-way junction where a convenience store is located.

Continue the hike by turning left (away from Okpo Bay) at the three-way junction and proceed uphill all the way to the main Highway 14 junction. Cross the street, continuing uphill until you see the Admiral Hotel on your left about 100 meters away.

Guksabong Summit Loop via Aju-dong and DSME

N

Stone Steps

Stone Steps

P Start

Parking Lot

Trail Marker

Admiral Hotel

3-Way Junction

Steep

Guksabong 464m

Gazebo

Lookout Point

200m

300m

400m

100m

200m

300m

200m

100m

4-Way Junction Sign for Daewoo Apt.

Everville Apts.

DSME Shipyard

0   500m

Hike 63 `MODERATE`

The Okpo Admiral Hotel to Gohyeon SHI Hotel Route

⭐ **Rating:** Moderate

🔄 **Route Type:** Point to Point

🧍 **Distance:** 11 km

🕐 **Duration:** 5 hr

⛰️ **Elevation Gain:** 425 m

🛒 **Stroller Friendly:** No

🚩 **GPS START:** 34.890058, 128.686095 (at 200 m behind the Admiral Hotel, to the right and uphill)

🔺 **GPS SUMMIT:** 34.884822, 128.672168 (at Guksabong summit at 464 m)

🚩 **GPS FINISH:** 34.896042, 128.612077 (at the lobby of the Samsung Hotel)

 **HIKE DESCRIPTION**

This hike links Okpo and Gohyeon with the mountains that lie between these two main towns on the island. About 60 percent of this hike is on paved road/sidewalk and the remainder is on well-worn forest trails. Hikers will be rewarded with great views over both DSME and SHI Shipyards at the beginning and end of this hike.

You will start this hike at the same location as Hike 60 and proceed to the summits of Guksabong and Little Guksabong in the same way. From Little Guksabong, follow the trail as it winds below the rocky nub and bears to the northwest through a heavy pine forest and then rapidly descends. After about 500 meters, the trail crosses a gravel fire road and continues on the opposite side of the road through thicker forest for about 1 kilometer until it emerges onto a small paved road. From here, the remainder of the hike is paved (approximately 7 kilometers).

Continuing on, turn left and walk along the road downhill as it follows a stream bed on the right-hand side and passes many single-family homes and small kindergartens. As the valley opens up, rice paddies line the road, especially lovely in the summer and early autumn just before harvest, with deepening shades of green and yellow as the plants become heavy with rice grains.

Follow the road until you reach a bridge that crosses the stream. Do not cross the bridge; instead, follow the road on your left and walk along the stream. At the next intersection, do a short dogleg to your right for 20 meters and then left, skirting the Suwol Hillstate Apartment Complex on your right. At the next major intersection, turn right and again skirt the same complex on your right as you follow the sidewalk for the next 800 meters until you come to a large four-way junction (just past a small church about 50 meters before the junction). At this intersection you will turn left and proceed up a steep hill on the sidewalk, soon passing the Star Hill Apartments on your right and a megachurch on your left.

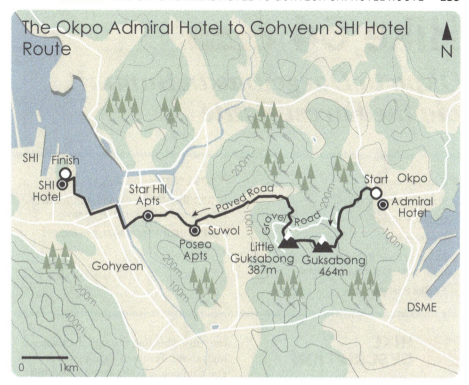

The Okpo Admiral Hotel to Gohyeun SHI Hotel Route

N

SHI Finish

SHI Hotel

Star Hill Apts

Paved Road

Start Okpo

Admiral Hotel

Gravel Road

Suwol

Poseo Apts

Little Guksabong 387m

Guksabong 464m

Gohyeon

DSME

0   1km

Continuing on, stay straight and descend a hill. At the bottom of the hill, merge with a road below and continue straight. Soon you will cross the main Gohyeon River by way of a bridge. After crossing the bridge, turn right and follow the river all the way to Hwy 14 Harbor Front Drive. At the intersection, turn left and walk all the way down to the four-way intersection opposite the shopping mall and then turn right, following the harbor (and reclamation works) on your right for about 500 meters. Enter the SHI Hotel on your right and in about 200 meters, take the side entrance of SHI Shipyard on your right.

Now, turn left and enter the large parking lot in front of the SHI Hotel and take the stairway behind the main building as it quickly climbs the bluff up to the modern red brick Samsung Hotel. Follow the final 200 meters of roadway to your left as it winds around to end at the lobby entrance of the hotel.

Hike 64 `MODERATE`

Okpo to Daegeumsan Summit via the Forest Route

- ⭐ **Rating:** Moderate
- 〰 **Route Type:** Out and Back
- 📍 **Distance:** 14 km
- 🕐 **Duration:** 6 hr
- 🏔 **Elevation Gain:** 200 m (most of the gain occurs in the final 750 m to the summit)
- 🍼 **Stroller Friendly:** No

- 🚩 **GPS START:** 34.904421, 128.687291
- 🔺 **GPS SUMMIT:** 34.951662, 128.700011 (at Daegeumsan summit at 437.5 m)
- 🚩 **GPS FINISH:** 34.904421, 128.687291

HIKE DESCRIPTION

This day hike is less popular than some of the others, allowing you to be alone in nature, with birds singing in the trees and the wind whistling through the treetops high above. Frequent sightings of deer and wild boar are also common on this trail. The entire route offers rare glimpses of the ocean to the east and the inland hills to the west as it follows the ridgeline

Okpo to Daegeumsan Summit via the Forest Route

N

Daegeumsan
437.5m

East Sea

Deokpo

Start

Okpo

0   2km

north all the way to Daegeumsan, the farthest north of the "11 Famous Peaks of Geoje." The trail is relatively level and follows the gentle rise and fall of the ridgeline, with the exception of the initial ascent up to the ridge and the final push to the summit.

You will start by passing along some newly developed villas at the very top of Okpo, with views across Okpo all the way to DSME Shipyard and Okneyobong towering above Okpo Bay. Continuing on, the concrete fire road quickly becomes a dirt road and foot trail until it joins a wide fire road at the ridgeline proper. From here, you will follow the ridgeline as it crosses the main Hwy 58 tunnel, with views out toward sparkling Deokpo Beach and over Deokpo Valley, dotted with homes, apartment buildings, and fields in between. The Hwy 58 viaduct bridge, in the early part of the hike, is also an impressive sight.

Continuing on the trail, you will enter a very peaceful part of the island, skirting the ocean to the east and small farms and the northern reservoir to the west. About 1.4 kilometers before the summit, you will encounter a fire road crossing the trail. Continue straight, and in 500 meters merge onto a fire road. Turn left here and follow the road for 100 meters until arriving at another fire road. Cross this road and begin the final 750-meter climb up the steep trail to the summit of Daegeumsan, about 25 meters to your right after emerging out of the forest.

A large rock marker and an adjacent rock cairn clearly mark the summit of Daegeumsan, which offers views in all directions. A small gazebo shelter lies an additional 25 meters south of the summit. Rest here before you backtrack to Okpo to complete this hike.

Hike 65 MODERATE

Okneyobong Summit Route

⭐ **Rating:** Moderate

🔄 **Route Type:** Out and Back

📍 **Distance:** 5.6 km

🕐 **Duration:** 2–3 hr

🏔 **Elevation Gain:** 475 m

🛒 **Stroller Friendly:** No

🚩 **GPS START:** 34.862200, 128.690642 (at the parking lot above Aju-dong Stadium)

🔺 **GPS SUMMIT:** 34.852308, 128.693446 (at Okneyobong summit at 554.7 m)

🚩 **GPS FINISH:** 34.862200, 128.690642

HIKE DESCRIPTION

Okneyobong towers over Okpo Bay and DSME. It is the third-highest peak on Geoje and offers amazing views from its lofty summit. For this hike, you will start in Aju-dong at the parking lot above the stadium and adjacent to the YWCA building. On the southwestern edge of the

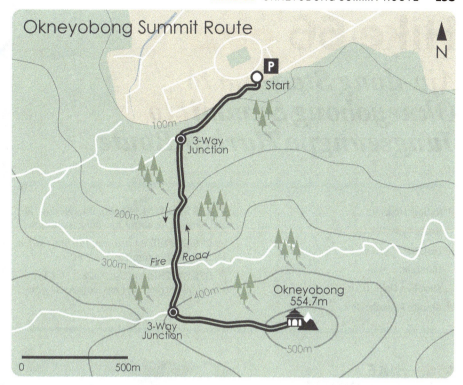

Okneyobong Summit Route

N

Start

P

100m

3-Way
Junction

200m

300m   Fire Road

400m

Okneyobong
554.7m

3-Way
Junction

500m

0   500m

parking lot, you will see a boot-cleaning station. Take the dirt path up the hill into the forest.

First, you will pass a few family gardens. Bear to the right heading westward. After a short while you will emerge into a clearing with outdoor gym equipment. The trail has an option to continue straight or turn to the left and head uphill. Take the trail to the left.

The trail will become quite steep in places, and you will continue to gain elevation until you reach a fire road about two-thirds of the way to the ridgeline. Cross the fire road and climb the small steel steps to continue the hike to the ridgeline, where you will emerge from the heavy forest into a marshy clearing full of reeds and high grass.

At this clearing you have the option of going right or left as the trail merges with

a ridgeline trail. Turn left and continue uphill toward the summit. You will pass a clearing with the markings for a now-defunct helicopter pad before you again pass into deeper forest. Here you will continue to climb higher and higher, heading eastward along the ridgeline. Soon a concrete blockhouse and cables will come into view, along with antennas and a steel tower. The path dips to the left and skirts below these buildings before leveling off in a sunny clearing atop the mountain.

In the large clearing you will first pass a nice gazebo shelter, and then 25 meters farther the stone marker at the summit may be found on a small rocky outcrop. Make sure to take a rest at the summit, enjoying the magnificent vistas from the top, especially to the north over DSME and Okpo, all the way to the mainland and Pusan Port. After a rest, backtrack to the parking lot on the same route to complete the hike.

Hike 66 MODERATE

Aju-dong Stadium to Okneyobong Summit to Jangseungpo Harbor Route

★ **Rating:** Moderate

〰 **Route Type:** Point to Point

👣 **Distance:** 7 km

🕐 **Duration:** 3–4 hr

⛰ **Elevation Gain:** 475 m

🛒 **Stroller Friendly:** No

🚩 **GPS START:** 34.862200, 128.690642 (at the parking lot above Aju-dong Stadium)

🔺 **GPS SUMMIT:** 34.852308, 128.693446 (at Okneyobong summit at 554.7 m)

🚩 **GPS FINISH:** 34.866913, 128.724454 (at the hotel entrance below Geoje Arts Center)

📖 HIKE DESCRIPTION

This half-day hike starts at the same point as Hike 65 but continues down the ridge to the east and northeast, stopping by a fifteenth-century smoke tower monument and ending in the bustling fishing port of Jangseungpo.

Following the Hike 65 details, from the Okneyobong summit marker continue on the trail to the east as it rapidly descends the southern ridge toward a temple. However, pay careful attention for a trail, which branches off to your left when the junction is met (after a 100-meter drop below the ridgeline). Take the left turn and follow this new trail. Do not descend to the temple.

The trail will pass through the forest and offer occasional views over the sprawling DSME Shipyard to the north and over Jisepo and the Daemyung Resort to the south. An especially nice view can be

Aju-dong Stadium to Okneyobong
Summit to Jangseungpo Harbor Route

N

found looking south from a rocky outcrop above the highway tunnel entrance, which lies far below.

Continuing on, you will soon arrive in a clearing with a WC and a historical marker for the large smoke tower, which has been dutifully rebuilt to its former glory. Enjoy views all along the coastline to the east and across the DSME Shipyard to the hills of the island's interior. From the smoke tower monument, descend via a fire road heading east until you pass some gym equipment. A staircase will emerge on your left; take this down to the street and cross the highway to the opposite sidewalk.

Once on the sidewalk, turn to your left and follow it all the way to the road just before the Geoje Arts Center, where you will turn right and head downhill to the harbor front drive. At the harbor front, turn left and continue about 100 meters

to the Home4Rest Hotel. From here, take a taxi back to the start point, a short 10-minute drive.

Hike 67 DIFFICULT

Double Summit Traverse Loop

⭐ **Rating:** Difficult

〰️ **Route Type:** Loop

📍 **Distance:** 16 km

🕐 **Duration:** 6–8 hr

⛰️ **Elevation Gain:** 700 m

👶 **Stroller Friendly:** No

🚩 **GPS START:** 34.883197, 128.612546 (same as Hike 56)

🔺 **GPS SUMMIT:** 34.870367, 128.608234 (at Gyeryongsan summit at 566 m)

🔺 **GPS SUMMIT:** 34.839957, 128.630252 (at Seonjasan summit at 507 m)

🚩 **GPS FINISH:** 34.883197, 128.612546

📖 HIKE DESCRIPTION

This hike is a grand exploration of the mountain ridge separating Geoje-Myeon to the west and Gohyeon (aka "Geoje City") to the northeast. The range runs from the northwest toward the southeast and encompasses two of the "11 Famous Peaks of Geoje." You will start the hike at the same place as Hike 56 and follow the route all the way to the monorail observation platform, passing Gyeryong-san, the first peak on this hike. Do not descend at this point, but go straight,

following the concrete fire road to the southeast for about 600 meters until it merges with a dirt/gravel fire road. At the merger, turn to your left and continue about 450 meters until you reach a saddle with a grassy field on your right and a small shelter/helipad just beyond it. After taking a rest at the shelter, pass the vehicle gate and follow the well-defined trail all the way to Seonjasan, the second summit.

After bagging Seonjasan, backtrack to the shelter and turn right onto the fire road. Proceed for about 400 meters, paying close attention to the left side of the road as you look for a trail entrance. When you find the trail, turn left. The trail rapidly descends through the forest to a junction with a fire road adjacent to a large parking lot on your right. Turn left, with the parking lot behind you, and follow the fire road until you merge with the trail you used at the beginning of the hike to reach the summit of Gyeryongsan. At this point, turn right and leave the fire road, rejoining the trail as it passes down the slope, across the Bypass Highway footbridge, and beside the vegetable plots back to the parking area.

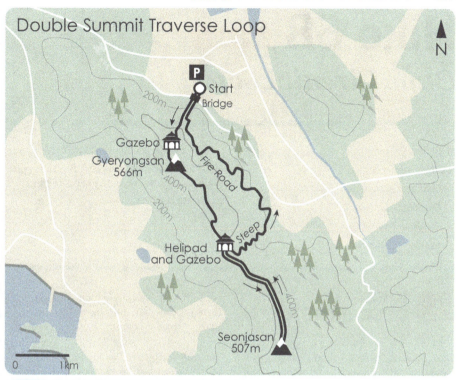

Double Summit Traverse Loop

P
○ Start
Bridge
200m
Gazebo
Gyeryongsan
566m
Fire Road
400m
200m
Steep
Helipad
and Gazebo
400m
Seonjasan
507m
N
0   1km

Hike 68 DIFFICULT

Okpo Circuit Loop

- ★ **Rating:** Difficult
- **Route Type:** Loop
- **Distance:** 21 km
- **Duration:** 8–10 hr
- ▲ **Elevation Gain:** 900 m
- **Stroller Friendly:** No

GPS START: 34.904421, 128.687291
▲ **GPS SUMMIT:** 34.884822, 128.672168 (at Guksabong summit at 464 m)
GPS FINISH: 34.904421, 128.687291

HIKE DESCRIPTION

This hike takes a circular route around Okpo, taking in the Deokpo Valley, Deokpo Beach, Okpo coastal track, Okpo/DSME harbor front, and the forested ascent to the rocky summit of Guksabong. Enjoy pristine forest walks where you will barely run into another soul, and views from atop the mountain's rocky cliffs and summit as hawks circle high above in the fresh salty air, along with fun "urban hiking" through Okpo.

You will start this amazing loop hike at the same location as Hike 64. Hike up onto the ridge in the same manner, passing over the Hwy 58 tunnel for about 200 meters while keeping a close eye on the right-hand side of the trail for a downslope trail to the Deokpo Valley

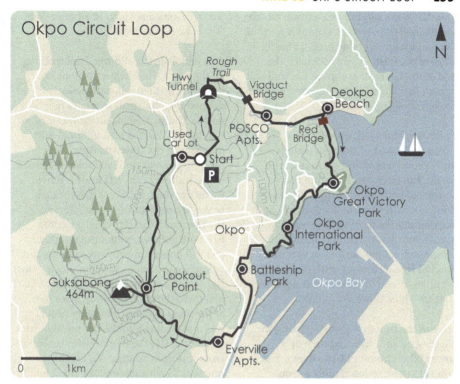

Okpo Circuit Loop

N

floor. **(Note: This area can be slightly overgrown, so take the best looking of the many trails.)** Once on the main road, turn right and proceed under the highway viaduct bridge. Follow the road all the way to POSCO Apartments, which you will pass on your right as you follow the road. You will come to a T-junction; turn left and follow along the creek, which flows along the right-hand side. Continue to follow the creek as it makes its way to Deokpo Beach.

Take a rest on the beach before backtracking to the mouth of the creek, where you will see a red steel bridge. Cross the bridge and take the stairs on the opposite side to the coastal track trail, which will follow the coastline all the way to the Okpo fishing harbor. En route, you will pass behind the Okpo Great Victory Park. Some of the track will be on a forested trail, some on concrete/village corniche, and some of it on faux-wood boardwalk. Keep the bay

on your left-hand side, and you will reach Okpo fishing harbor. Skirt the perimeter of the harbor to the west and then head south following the sidewalks to the west side of the blue glass DSME buildings. You will pass several convenience stores and the full-size replica of a turtle ship (see Hike 53 for details).

Continue to follow the sidewalk south along the perimeter of the DSME Shipyard until you come to the main highway road junction. Cross the main road and continue straight for 50 meters, following the small road to the west and then sharply south. Follow this road past low-rise apartments for about 200 meters until you reach the next four-way intersection. At this junction, turn right and proceed about 150 meters west, passing a supermarket on your right, and then turn left at a roundabout. Proceed 75 meters until you see a series of steps that lead up to the forested hill beyond.

Take the steps and follow the trail, passing the Everville Apartment Complex on your left and many vegetable plots on both sides of the trail. As you approach the end of the Everville complex, the trail will appear to split. Take the trail that bears to the left, heading uphill.

Following this trail, quickly pass through the last of the vegetable plots and several tree stumps. Once in the forest, the trees quickly mute the sounds of traffic and shipyard clamor. Soon you will hear the birds again and see chipmunks darting here and there across your path. The elevation will continue to climb, and soon you will emerge into a clearing with outdoor gym equipment and a shelter with a platform that provides views over Okpo.

Follow the trail to the west, passing the clearing on your left, and then uphill toward the summit of Guksabong. You will gain in elevation rapidly as you make for the rocky peak ahead. Staying on the trail, you will pass a few enticing overlooks on rocky outcrops and will glimpse distant views through the thick forest, but wait until you reach the top for the truly amazing views in all directions (see Hike 60 for details).

Descend from the summit, backtracking all the way to the shelter overlook near the clearing, then follow the clearly defined ridgeline trail as it goes in a northerly direction for about 750 meters. Stay on the trail for an additional 400 meters past the "Daewoo Apts" sign, heading straight until you reach a branch in the trail. Take the left branch down to the fire road, NOT the right branch to the fire station. Once you intersect the fire road, turn right and continue in a northerly direction until eventually you will pass an apartment complex and emerge onto a small, paved roadway. Turn right on this road and follow it about 60 meters to the main highway. Turn right at the main highway and proceed for about 200 meters to the intersection with stoplights. Use the crosswalk to carefully cross this rather dangerous and busy junction. Having crossed the road, follow the sidewalk, which skirts along the southern edge of a used car dealership. Continue straight, and in about 450 meters you will reach the starting point for this epic day hike.

Hike 69 VERY DIFFICULT

North-South Island Traverse

⭐ **Rating:** Very Difficult

🔄 **Route Type:** Point to Point

📍 **Distance:** 58 km

🕐 **Duration:** 26 hr (includes an overnight at Simwonsa Temple)

⛰ **Elevation Gain:** 3,700 m

🛒 **Stroller Friendly:** No

🚩 **GPS START:** 34.956152, 128.691111 (at the Daegeumsan parking lot)

🔺 **GPS SUMMIT:** 34.951662, 128.700011 (at Daegeumsan summit at 437.5 m)

🔺 **GPS SUMMIT:** 34.884822, 128.672168 (at Guksabong summit at 464 m)

🔺 **GPS SUMMIT:** 34.852308, 128.693446 (at Okneyobong summit at 554.7 m)

🔺 **GPS SUMMIT:** 34.822537, 128.656575 (at Bookbyeongsan summit at 465.4 m)

🔺 **GPS SUMMIT:** 34.784405, 128.616165 (at Nojosan summit at 565 m)

🔺 **GPS SUMMIT:** 34.754224, 128.622031 (at Garasan summit at 585 m)

🔺 **GPS SUMMIT:** 34.714041, 128.601316 (at Mangsan summit at 397 m)

🏁 **GPS FINISH:** 34.726008, 128.603156 (at the Myeongsa Beach parking lot)

HIKE DESCRIPTION

This epic traverse from the north to the south of Geoje takes in seven of the "11 Famous Peaks of Geoje" in a 2-day period of intense hiking, with overnight camping at Simwonsa Temple. Like Hike 88, this hike is largely made up of full or partial sections of previous hikes in this book; however, there are some "virgin" sections yet untouched by your muddy boots, so add them all up and get going!

Start at the humble parking lot at the western edge of Daegeumsan, as per Hike 47. After making the summit of Daegeumsan, you will then walk to Okpo, following the route (in reverse) of Hike 64. Next is a portion of Hike 68 (in reverse), following the trail all the way to the overlook just below Guksabong. At this point, carefully search for the (less than clearly marked)

trail heading not toward Aju-dong but instead toward Okneyobong. Stay southbound and do not leave the ridgeline. You will find the trail (even if you need to do a little scrambling).

Note: In a pinch, it can help to hike over toward Little Guksabong first (see Hike 60, then at the saddle between the two summits, scramble down the southern scree-covered slope to the fire road below. Once at the fire road, turn left toward the east and follow the road about 500 meters until you intercept the ridgeline trail. Turn right and continue toward Okneyobong.

Continuing on, you will hike in a dense forest and enjoy some solitude until you pass over the top of the highway tunnel running between Okpo and Suwol. In about 1.5 kilometers, you will reach the four-way junction and small shelter, as

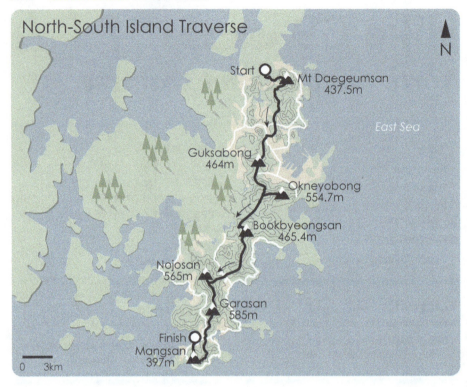

North-South Island Traverse

Start

Mt Daegeumsan
437.5m

East Sea

Guksabong
464m

Okneyobong
554.7m

Bookbyeongsan
465.4m

Nojosan
565m

Garasan
585m

Finish
Mangsan
397m

0   3km

N

noted in Hike 62. At this junction, go straight and stay on the trail heading toward Okneyobong. After about 2 kilometers, the trail will switch from a southbound direction to a sharp eastward direction. You will backtrack to this point after bagging Okneyobong.

Having made the summit of Okneyobong, backtrack to the point mentioned above, and then search for the lesser-used trail. Head south along the ridgeline **(Note: A fire road will pick up along this trail for some of the ridgeline)** until you emerge onto the paved mountain pass road linking Jisepo with the interior of the island. At this stage, turn right and follow the road about 300–400 meters until you see a small concrete bridge crossing the stream that snakes along the road and a metal sign with the Buddhist manja (backwards swastika) design. Cross the bridge and follow the road up toward Simwonsa Temple (see Hike 80).

As you hike up this small temple road, you will pass two flat gravel parking lots on your left-hand side, just 300 meters before you reach Simwonsa Temple. The lower parking lot acts as a windbreak, and there is a small stream just 10 meters beyond the eastern side of the parking lot perimeter. This is a great place to set up camp (but do make sure to be respectful of the site, practicing "leave no trace," and leave a donation for the monks and caretakers at the temple).

At night, revel in the dark skies overhead and the forest sounds as you fall asleep after a solid day of hiking. Aim to get up just before sunrise if you want to complete the rest of the trail in daylight. Having packed up camp, hike up the road from the parking lot to Simwonsa Temple and then follow the same route as noted in Hike 88 all the way to the finish point. Well done!

South Geoje

Hike 70 `EASY`

Dundeokgiseong Fortress Ruins and Woodubong Summit Route

⭐ **Rating:** Easy

🔁 **Route Type:** Out and Back

📍 **Distance:** 11 km

🕐 **Duration:** 4 hr

⛰️ **Elevation Gain:** 400 m

🛒 **Stroller Friendly:** No (however, there is a paved road from the start point up to the fortress that is stroller friendly)

🚩 **GPS START:** 34.857397, 128.512823

🔺 **GPS SUMMIT:** 34.870052, 128.505605 (at Woodubong summit at 445m)

🚩 **GPS FINISH:** 34.857397, 128.512823

 ## HIKE DESCRIPTION

On this hike near the western coast of Geoje, you can experience the slower-paced agricultural side of the island, which many visitors may miss. After finding a parking spot, either in the village or on the side of the main highway adjacent to the church, proceed on foot through the village, sticking to the main road and following signs for the fortress as you proceed uphill. After about 1.2 kilometers the road will bear off to the right and soon after begin a series of serpentine zigzags as it climbs up to the ridgeline where the fortress is located. The fortress site is very large (with numerous informational signboards in both Hangul and English) and the views are also impressive. From here you can see the valley in the east with Sanbangsan's rocky peak (standing at 507 meters) dominating the background, and west-northwest toward Tongyeong you can see many islands and fishing operations in the narrow waterway between Geoje and the mainland.

Having departed the fortress, proceed about 150 meters to the northeast until you come to a clearing and small dirt parking lot. On your right you will see a sign with a trail map for reaching the summit of Woodubong. After following this trail for 400 meters, you will pass a gazebo rest stop. Soon after, make the summit, which affords nice views along the length of the valley far below. Retracing your steps, return through the village to your start point.

Note: This hike can be made shorter by simply driving to the fortress and then hiking to the summit on the 600-meter trail that starts about 150 meters to the northeast of the fortress entrance gate. Alternatively, if you enjoy bushwhacking, there is a rather overgrown trail from the village to the first main turn in the serpentine road that will shave a good 4 kilometers off the route (round trip)—although your progress may be slow!

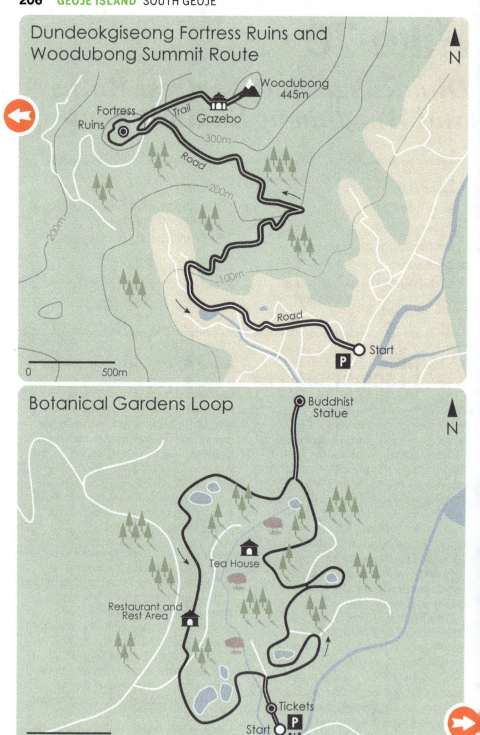

Dundeokgiseong Fortress Ruins and Woodubong Summit Route

N

Woodubong
445m

Gazebo

Fortress
Ruins

Trail

300m

Road

200m

200m

100m

Road

Start

P

0   500m

Botanical Gardens Loop

Buddhist
Statue

N

Tea House

Restaurant and
Rest Area

Tickets

Start

P

0   100m

Hike 71 EASY

Botanical Gardens Loop

⭐ **Rating:** Easy

〰 **Route Type:** Loop

🧭 **Distance:** 750 m

🕐 **Duration:** 1–2 hr

⛰ **Elevation Gain:** 25 m

🛒 **Stroller Friendly:** Yes (but there are occasional steps and some hard-packed dirt/gravel pathways)

🚩 **GPS START:** 34.859186, 128.527025 (at the parking lot)

📍 **GPS POINT:** 34.862489, 128.527299 (at Buddhist statue at the gardens' highest point)

🚩 **GPS FINISH:** 34.859186, 128.527025 (at the parking lot)

📖 HIKE DESCRIPTION

The Geoje Botanical Gardens are a real treat for nature and plant lovers. Starting at the parking lot (which has a WC), pass the gate, following the trail that bears to the right and heads slightly uphill. A series of ponds, greenhouses, rare plants, and sculptures are interspersed with benches and swings. You will pass a tea house and continue upslope until you reach a Buddhist statue at the high point of the gardens, just below the edge of the forested hill. Now you start to head downhill, passing a small pond with silver reeds and the tea house. Make your way to a two-story building with a lovely restaurant and outdoor seating that provides a grand view of the gardens and the rocky summit of Sangbangsan, towering above the valley. After enjoying the view, make your way past more gardens until you reach the lotus pond. Cross the small bridge and turn right, and you will see the parking lot ahead.

Hike 72 `EASY`

Mundong Falls Route

- ⭐ **Rating:** Easy
- **Route Type:** Out and Back
- **Distance:** 1.8 km
- 🕐 **Duration:** 1 hr
- **Elevation Gain:** 75 m
- **Stroller Friendly:** Yes (but be prepared for a few steep stretches as you approach the falls)

- **GPS START:** 34.856649, 128.659749 (at the parking lot)
- ▲ **GPS SUMMIT:** 34.860453, 128.664440 (at Mundong Falls)
- **GPS FINISH:** 34.856649, 128.659749

📖 HIKE DESCRIPTION

This hike is a local favorite. It starts in the parking lot (there is a WC at the end of the parking lot adjacent to the forest and a small store and coffee shop near the beginning of the trail) and runs entirely on a paved surface all the way to the Mundong Falls. The best time to visit is following a day or two of heavy rain, as the falls can dry out significantly if it has been hot and sunny for a while. If it's been very wet for many days, this can also be an exciting time to visit, but don't be surprised to see a chaotic stream turned into a raging torrent with mild flooding in some places on the road. In such circumstances, be careful to watch the flow and depth of water and keep children away from the creek. Also expect that you will be coming home drenched from the wild falls! There are many nice places along the route to stop and have a picnic, and several platforms are set up near the creek for this activity. It's not unusual to find families resting under the shade of the trees, enjoying a picnic and an afternoon snooze while children play in the trickling creek

nearby. At the top of the road, adjacent to the waterfall, are several sets of outdoor gym equipment and some benches.

Mundong Falls Route

Hike 73 EASY
Windy Hill Loop

⭐ **Rating:** Easy

🔄 **Route Type:** Loop

📍 **Distance:** 2 km

🕐 **Duration:** 2 hr

⛰ **Elevation Gain:** 70 m

🛒 **Stroller Friendly:** Yes (but there are some stairs from the parking lot up to the windmill)

🚩 **GPS START:** 34.742174, 128.662867 (at the ferry parking lot)

🔺 **GPS SUMMIT:** 34.743382, 128.663334 (at the windmill)

🚩 **GPS FINISH:** 34.742174, 128.662867

 HIKE DESCRIPTION

All the local tourist pamphlets for Geoje Island seem to have a picture of the replica Dutch-style windmill that calls Windy Hill home. Despite the crowds, Windy Hill is a lovely place to enjoy a short stroll with the kids and enjoy expansive views across the bay toward the coastal range running north and south along the rocky spine of Geoje, while also enjoying the fresh ocean breeze.

The hike starts at the busy parking lot for the ferry boats, which depart for the nearby Oedo (Botanical Island) and Haegeumgang (a rocky islet). From the parking lot, walk along the harbor front bearing to the northwest until the staircase leading up to the windmill comes into view on your right. **(Note: Despite these stairs, the remainder of the hike is stroller friendly.)** Once you have passed the stairs, follow the trail north toward the small lighthouse to enjoy the magnificent views and rest at the benches in the open grassy area. The sea breeze sweeps across this rocky spit and the waves crash on the rocks below, making this a relaxing place to spend some time—assuming the crowds are not too bothersome! Moving from the lighthouse point, proceed up the gradual rise toward

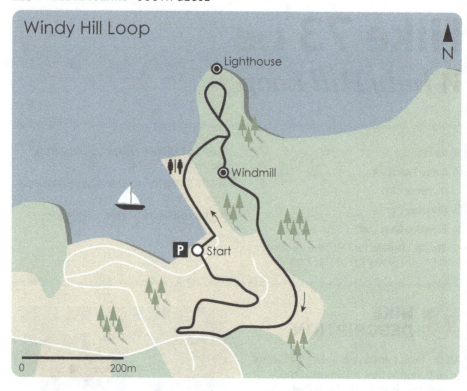

Windy Hill Loop

the replica Dutch windmill. Then carry on along the trail to the southeast as it cuts through a forest and eventually bears to the west, joining the roadway. Follow the road to the west until you reach the first paved road on your left and follow this as it zigzags back down the hill through the village to the parking lot.

Hike 74 `EASY`

Fortress Ruins and Gun Point Overlook Loop via Gujora Beach

⭐ **Rating:** Easy

🔄 **Route Type:** Loop

📍 **Distance:** 4.5 km

🕐 **Duration:** 3 hr

⛰ **Elevation Gain:** 130 m

🛒 **Stroller Friendly:** No

🚩 **GPS START:** 34.809026, 128.690800 (at the Gujora Beach parking lot)

🔺 **GPS SUMMIT:** 34.799018, 128.695972 (gazebo at summit, 146 m)

🚩 **GPS FINISH:** 34.809026, 128.690800

 ## HIKE DESCRIPTION

This hike offers many nice diversions and views along the way. Start from the Gujora Beach parking lot with its views out to sea past a golden stretch of sand. Take the stairs down to the beach roadway and turn left. Walk along the beach following the curve of the bay. The beach road becomes a concrete corniche road where the rocky foreshore begins. After about 750 meters there is a trail marker for a trail that goes up the hill to your left.

It may seem that you are walking through a private vegetable patch at first, but stay on the trail and all will be well. You will pass through a tunnel of bamboo and after a minute emerge onto higher ground, which offers a nice view back toward the beach. After a few more minutes, some outdoor gym equipment will come into view as you stay on the trail and keep heading in a southerly direction. Soon you will come to a reconstructed fortress wall and a historical marker providing details.

Proceed to the southerly end of the wall and then round it and turn left 90 degrees to the east-northeast.

At this point a grand view of the Wahyeon Peninsula across the bay opens up in front of you. Continue to the edge of the stone wall ruins and carefully follow the wall along the southern edge of the ruins as you descend the hill. At the bottom you will merge with a trail going to the right and left. First go to the left about 50 meters, where you will find a large tree with many colorful streamers flying from it and a small shaman's shrine with Buddhist artwork within.

After visiting the shrine, backtrack to the junction and continue going straight. You will cross a small wooden bridge. Bear to your left and follow the trail in a southerly direction once more. A side trail with a marker indicating a stone beach will come up on your left. Pass this and carry on straight as the trail climbs through the forest and gains elevation. Suddenly the trail will bear to the right up a few steps. Off to your left is a camouflaged army blockhouse.

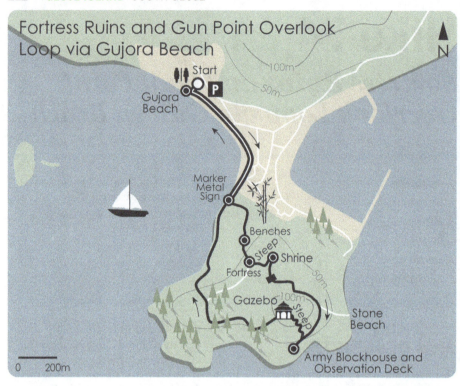

Fortress Ruins and Gun Point Overlook Loop via Gujora Beach

Stop here to explore the small army museum and then follow the trail on the other side of the blockhouse down to a cliffside observation deck and pillbox, also painted in camouflage. Look out for any army helmets left lying around!

After enjoying the amazing views out to sea, backtrack up the hill to the block-house and rejoin the main trail, which now becomes quite steep with several serpentine curves and steps as it climbs up to the highest point on the peninsula. As you approach the summit, the forest gives way to a huge clearing atop the hill, which offers a large platform, benches, and a small gazebo shelter. Many lovely views can be had from this vantage point, both out to sea and back toward Gujora Beach.

Continue on the hike by crossing the summit and following the path downhill through heavy forest. At one point you will come to a junction. Bear to your left

and skirt along a meadow as you head toward the southwest. Eventually, you will come to another junction with a small raised platform. You will see a well-de-fined trail to the right (which heads back to the fortress ruins) or to the left and downhill. For this hike, you will head downhill, where the trail will soon merge back onto the concrete bay road along the shoreline. At this point, follow the road all the way back to Gujora Beach parking lot to complete the loop.

Note: Gujora is one of many beaches on Geoje where camping is very popular. It has both a WC and running water available.

Hike 75 EASY

Wayheon Peninsula Smoke Tower and Dolphin Overlook Route

- ⭐ **Rating:** Easy
- 〽 **Route Type:** Out and Back
- 🧭 **Distance:** 6.5 km
- 🕐 **Duration:** 4–5 hr
- ⛰ **Elevation Gain:** 290 m
- 🛒 **Stroller Friendly:** No

- 🚩 **GPS START:** 34.800212, 128.715001 (at the parking lot)
- 🔺 **GPS SUMMIT:** 34.798925, 128.724598 (at the smoke tower)
- 🏁 **GPS FINISH:** 34.800212, 128.715001

HIKE DESCRIPTION

The Gonggoji area on the eastern coast of the island is famous in Geoje and full of visitor attractions. For this hike, you will begin at the parking lot, which commands a magnificent view of the fishing harbor. There is always something of interest going on in the parking lot with fishermen repairing nets, boats, etc.

Start by walking to the southernmost end of the parking lot, then cross the road and bear left up the very steep concrete road. Continue on this road past pensions and a shelter, and soon you will arrive at the top where the roadway stops. The path continues to your left. Stay on this path heading straight, and it will slowly head downhill until you cross a stream and join what appears to be a fire road. As the fire road begins to slope upward there will be a sign for the Dolphin Overlook and rope-covered fence poles on your right. Turn right. Stay on the trail until you emerge from the forest onto a wooden platform atop a high

rocky cliff overlooking the sea. The fresh sea air and the sound of the waves crashing far below is a relaxing and soul-stirring experience.

After you have enjoyed a moment of zen, leave the overlook and bear right up the steep hill until you reach the fire road. At the fire road, turn right and continue until you hit the junction with a paved roadway. Across from this junction is a helpful map of the Wayheon Peninsula. At this point, turn left and hike along the paved road until you come to a sign and path for the smoke tower on the left-hand side.

Turn left and head uphill, continuing as it gets steeper, until you break through the trees and are rewarded with a magnificent view of the smoke tower ruins. A small plaque explains the historical points associated with the ruins. The well-worn path continues along the sharp rocks to the top of the ruins, where you can enjoy a 360-degree view of Geoje's eastern coast from 290 meters up. Afterward, backtrack on the route to the parking lot.

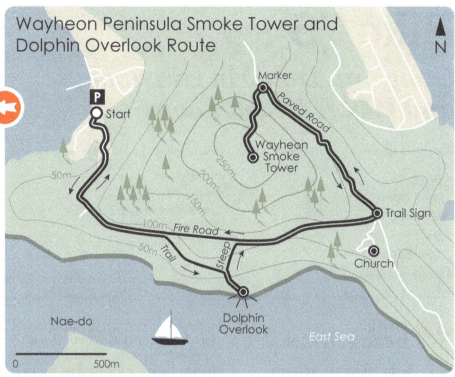

Wayheon Peninsula Smoke Tower and Dolphin Overlook Route

N

Marker

Paved Road

Wayheon
Smoke
Tower

Trail Sign

P
Start

50m

250m

200m

150m

100m Fire Road

50m Trail

Steep

Church

Nae-do

Dolphin
Overlook

East Sea

0   500m

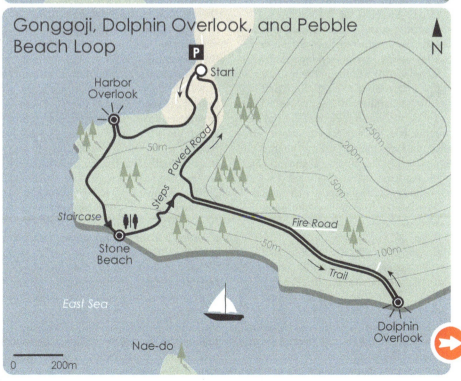

Gonggoji, Dolphin Overlook, and Pebble Beach Loop

N

P
Start

Harbor
Overlook

50m

Paved Road

Steps

Staircase

Stone
Beach

Fire Road

50m

100m

250m

200m

150m

Trail

East Sea

Nae-do

Dolphin
Overlook

0   200m

Hike 76 `EASY`

Gonggoji, Dolphin Overlook, and Pebble Beach Loop

⭐ **Rating:** Easy

〰️ **Route Type:** Loop

📏 **Distance:** 5.5 km

🕐 **Duration:** 3–4 hr

⛰️ **Elevation Gain:** 150 m

🛒 **Stroller Friendly:** No

🚩 **GPS START:** 34.800212, 128.715001 (at the parking lot)

🔺 **GPS SUMMIT:** 34.792368, 128.723525 (at the Dolphin Overlook)

🏁 **GPS FINISH:** 34.800212, 128.715001

HIKE DESCRIPTION

You will begin this hike at the same parking lot as Hike 75. Walk to the southernmost end of the parking lot, cross the road, and bear right and then uphill, passing under a small wooden arbor with a curved top. Continue on the trail and you will soon come to a sign for a path heading downhill to the right, which leads to a nice overlook. Once you have enjoyed this side trip, backtrack to the main path and turn right to continue on the trail. Soon the trail will emerge at the top of a metal staircase that you will descend to a pebble beach. Just opposite the beach is the island of Nae-do, only 500 meters away across a narrow strait.

Here, you can enjoy the relaxing sound of the waves mingling with the polished smooth rocks, which are great for skipping. At the top of the rocky beach there is a WC available. After enjoying the beach, head toward the WC building, where you will find a path heading into the forest to the right. Follow the path uphill past small, terraced fields of fruit bushes and trees. Soon you will emerge at the bottom of a large stone staircase closed in by beautiful camellia flowers. Head to the top of the stairs, enjoying the wildflowers, until the path turns off to the right. Follow this until it merges with a larger trail. At this junction with the larger trail, turn right. Go straight (it will slowly head downhill) until you cross a stream and join what appears to be a fire road. As the fire road begins to slope upward, there will be a sign for the Dolphin Overlook and rope-covered fence poles on your right. Turn right and take this path. Stay on the trail until you emerge from the forest onto a wooden platform atop a high rocky cliff. After you have enjoyed the views and maybe even sighted a dolphin or two, leave the overlook behind and backtrack until you reach the fire road again. At the fire road, turn left and stay on the trail, crossing the stream again and heading uphill until you come to a concrete road at the end of the trail on your right. Bear to the right and head downhill, following the road until you emerge at the bottom, just opposite the parking lot where you started the hike.

Hike 77 MODERATE

Sanbangsan Summit Loop

⭐ **Rating:** Moderate

🔄 **Route Type:** Loop

📍 **Distance:** 7 km

🕐 **Duration:** 3–4 hr

⛰️ **Elevation Gain:** 450 m

🛒 **Stroller Friendly:** No

🚩 **GPS START:** 34.859186, 128.527025 (at the Botanical Gardens parking lot)

🔺 **GPS SUMMIT:** 34.861590, 128.539013 (at Sanbangsan summit at 507 m)

🚩 **GPS FINISH:** 34.859186, 128.527025

HIKE DESCRIPTION

This is a lovely hike on the less-developed western side of Geoje, where you will enjoy pastoral valleys, lofty rock-studded peaks, and deep forests of pine. We begin at the same place as Hike 71: the parking lot of the Botanical Gardens. Looming directly over the parking lot to the east is the rocky pinnacle of Sanbangsan.

Leaving the parking lot and turning right, head downhill for about 400 meters until you come to a concrete fire road on your right. Turn right and follow the road as it passes fields and a home on your left before entering the forest. Continue to follow the road for about 3.5 kilometers as it gradually rises up the mountain, passing the Botanical Gardens on your right and gaining ever-better views of the surrounding countryside. The road ends in a grassy field that has a small WC on one side and a helipad and shelter 25 meters up and to your left. **(Note: The helipad is a great camping spot and is reachable by a vehicle with four-wheel drive.)**

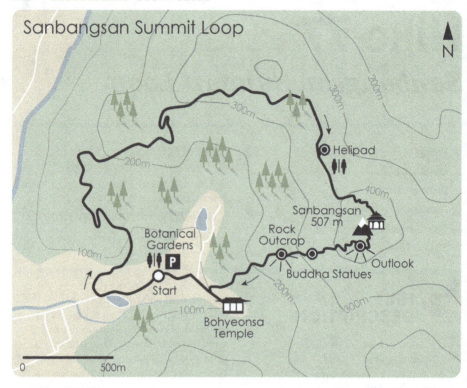

Sanbangsan Summit Loop

Continue the hike by following a foot trail as it passes the WC and proceeds into the forest proper. The trail will drop slightly, and soon you will arrive at a final steep push along the edge of the rocky cliffside. The trail has steps, chains, and ropes leading up to the summit, about 15 minutes farther on. As you near the summit, a small gazebo shelter on your left offers a respite from the steep climb. Continue about 25 meters farther to the summit, which offers 360-degree views at 507 meters above sea level.

Following a rest, proceed carefully on the trail to the east of the stone summit marker and pass down the rocky trail for about 75 meters. You will come to a split in the trail. Go straight for an additional 20 meters until you come to a large viewing platform. From the platform, backtrack 20 meters to the junction and head downhill on the trail to your left.

This next section of trail (1.2 kilometers) is quite steep. Be sure to maintain good control as you descend.

About 600 meters down the trail on your right, keep an eye out for a small cave that has three small Buddha statues inside. Continue downhill an additional 200 meters, where the trail opens up onto a rocky outcrop with a view of the valley spur below and its terraced rice paddies.

To finish the route, pass a small bench, proceed down the stairs, and follow the trail to the bottom until you emerge onto the road below. At this point, turn to your left and walk about 150 meters to the small temple complex of Bohyeonsa. After exploring the temple, backtrack to the road and follow it to the northwest, passing farmhouses and fields (and barking dogs) for about 450 meters until you arrive back at the Botanical Gardens parking lot.

Hike 78 MODERATE

Gohyeon/Gyeryongsan Fire Road Route

⭐ **Rating:** Moderate

🔁 **Route Type:** Out and Back

🥾 **Distance:** 17 km (8.5 km one way)

🕐 **Duration:** 5–6 hr

⛰ **Elevation Gain:** 250 m

🛒 **Stroller Friendly:** Yes (but you need an off-road type with larger wheels)

🚩 **GPS START:** 34.859632, 128.627226 (at parking area)

👁 **GPS OVERLOOK:** 34.884780, 128.597936 (at overlook)

📍 **GPS HELIPAD:** 34.856920, 128.618557 (at helipad)

HIKE DESCRIPTION

This is a good hike if you want to avoid walking in the forest or on muddy trails after a lot of rain. It really consists of two different types of hikes. The first one from the parking location to the overlook rambles along the side of the mountain to the overlook (round trip will be a nice 10-kilometer walk on a level dirt road). Meanwhile, the portion from the parking lot up to the helipad will climb up 250 meters in elevation with a round-trip distance of 7 kilometers. Both offer a chance to get some good exercise while enjoying views over Gohyeon and along the ridge of the mountains. Due to the large number of trails that crisscross this mountain range, any number of different loop hikes and similar combinations can be enjoyed from this humble fire road.

Note: Off-road strollers and mountain bikes are appropriate on these routes as well.

bhyeon/Gyeryongsan Fire Road Route

N

Overlook

Fire Road

200m

100m
200m
300m
400m
500m

300m

100m

200m

P
Start

Helipad

0   1km

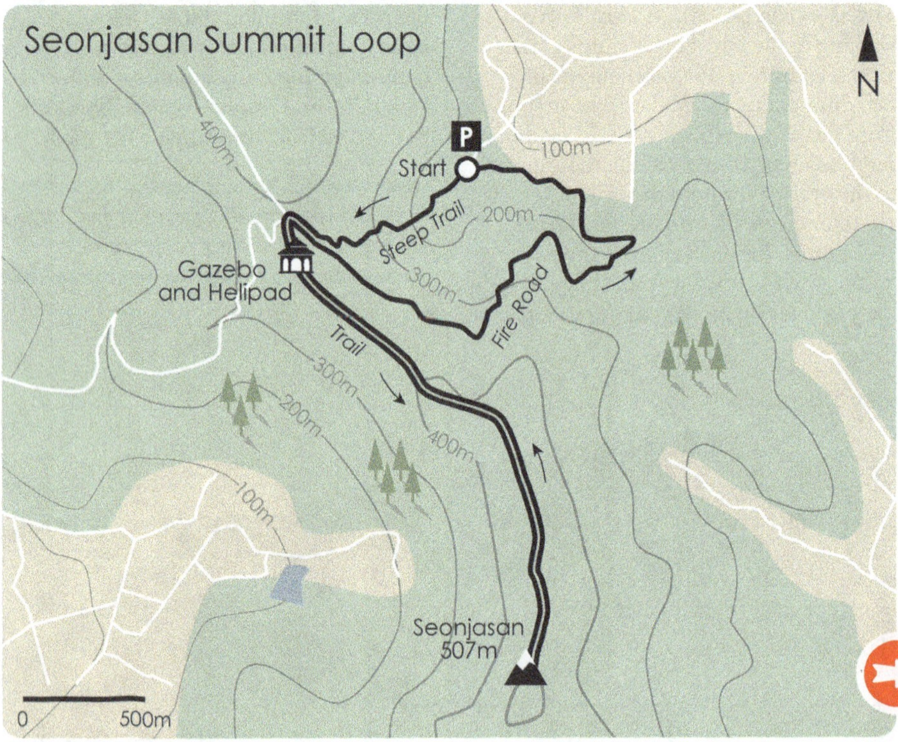

Seonjasan Summit Loop

N

400m

P
Start

100m

Steep Trail

200m

300m

Gazebo
and Helipad

Fire Road

Trail

300m

200m

400m

100m

Seonjasan
507m

0   500m

Hike 79 MODERATE

Seonjasan Summit Loop

★ **Rating:** Moderate

⌇ **Route Type:** Loop

📍 **Distance:** 9.2 km

🕐 **Duration:** 4 hr

⛰ **Elevation Gain:** 450 m

🛒 **Stroller Friendly:** No

🚩 **GPS START:** 34.859728, 128.627109 (at the parking lot)

🔺 **GPS SUMMIT:** 34.839957, 128.630252 (at Seonjasan summit at 507 m)

🚩 **GPS FINISH:** 34.859728, 128.627109

HIKE DESCRIPTION

This is a great hike on a forested ridgeline if you are looking to avoid the crowds on other trails. The hike starts at a paved parking lot that has a quiet, rocky stream passing below it. Looking at the creek uphill, walk to your right about 25 meters until you see a signpost and trail that heads up into the woods. The trail climbs steeply up the creek ravine and then zigzags up to the ridgeline to a gravel fire road.

When you emerge from the forest onto the fire road, turn to your right and continue about 200 meters to the saddle. At this point, proceed to the gazebo rest stop on your left, pass the helipad, and follow the trail past the meadow and into the forest in a southeasterly direction along the ridgeline.

This trail runs approximately 3 kilometers to the summit. Near the halfway point, you'll find a gazebo rest area. Farther along the trail, you will pass a few small thickets of closely spaced cedar trees that lie on the northern slope of the ridge, just about 800 meters before you emerge into a cleared summit area with a rock marker.

After enjoying the summit views, retrace your steps all the way back to the saddle adjacent to the helipad and first gazebo, and head down the fire road bearing southeast. Stay on the fire road as it zigzags, slowly descending the northern face of the mountain until it emerges back into the parking lot where you began the hike.

Note: In the summer you can find many fruiting fig trees along this fire road.

hike 80 `MODERATE`

Bookbyeongsan Summit Loop

- ★ **Rating:** Moderate
- **Route Type:** Loop
- **Distance:** 4.5 km
- ⏱ **Duration:** 3 hr
- **Elevation Gain:** 350 m
- **Stroller Friendly:** No

⚑ **GPS START:** 34.830446, 128.655009 (at the parking lot of Simwonsa Temple)

▲ **GPS SUMMIT:** 34.822537, 128.656575 (at Bookbyeongsan summit at 465.4 m)

⚑ **GPS FINISH:** 34.830446, 128.655009

HIKE DESCRIPTION

This hike starts at a peaceful little temple halfway up the mountainside.

After exploring Simwonsa Temple, head uphill following the dirt track. At the top of the rise, you will come to a three-way junction. Bear to the left and continue uphill. This section will

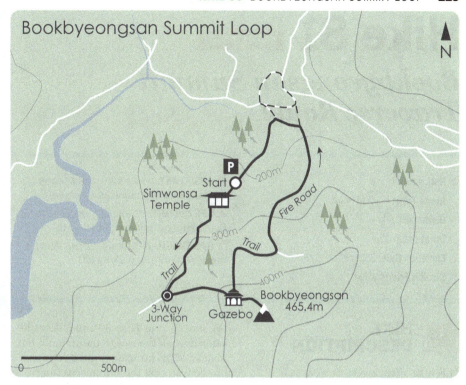

become a bit steep, but log stairs make the climb a bit easier. Eventually the steep trail will level off, and you will hike atop a forested ridgeline until you reach a small gazebo shelter. Follow the trail marker toward the summit (only 250 meters farther on). As you approach the summit, a small rocky "cave" will come into view on your left, followed by a short metal staircase.

From the summit marker, there are magnificent views in all directions, especially to the east toward the ocean. Proceed a little farther, and you will find a large rocky outcrop where you could put up a small tent if desired.

When ready, retrace your steps back to the small gazebo shelter. Bear to the right and take the trail through the woods, being careful to watch for a sharp turn to the right after about 300 meters. Soon you will start to descend a deforested slope. When you emerge onto a fire road, turn to your left and follow the road as it heads downhill.

Eventually you will pass a small clearing with high reeds on your left. At this point you can either: 1) continue on the fire road to the paved road, then bear to your left and walk a short distance until you reach the manja sign for Simwonsa Temple (this ancient Korean Buddhist symbol looks like a backwards swastika but has nothing to do with Nazi Germany), turn left again, and follow it back to the parking lot; or 2) hike through the reeds following the trail until it leads to a dirt road on the right, follow the road through the forest until it merges with the concrete temple road, turn left, and head uphill back to the temple.

ike 81 MODERATE

Bookbyeongsan Summit Traverse Route

⭐ **Rating:** Moderate

🔁 **Route Type:** Point to Point

👣 **Distance:** 2.9 km

🕐 **Duration:** 2–3 hr

⛰️ **Elevation Gain:** 350 m

🛒 **Stroller Friendly:** No

🚩 **GPS START:** 34.830446, 128.655009 (at the parking lot of Simwonsa Temple)

🔺 **GPS SUMMIT:** 34.822537, 128.656575 (Bookbyeongsan summit at 465.4 m)

🚩 **GPS FINISH:** 34.813399, 128.655696 (at the mountain pass parking lot)

HIKE DESCRIPTION

This hike offers lovely views as you scramble over rocky ridges and hike through light-growth forest with occasional views out to sea. Start off in the same way as Hike 80 and follow the same trail all the way to the summit, but instead of backtracking, you'll continue on the trail past the summit, passing the rocky outcrop and continuing along the ridgeline and over several more rocky outcrops (some which involve

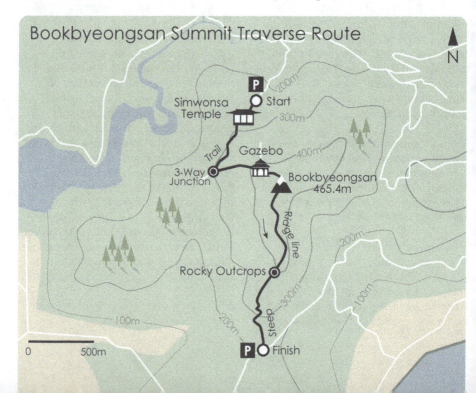

3-meter drops with ropes to assist in climbing down or up the rock face). In the final 600 meters, this hike begins a steep decent to the mountain pass road.

There's a large parking lot along the roadway and a map showing adjacent trails. If you wish to do this trail out and back, you can.

Hike 82 MODERATE

Nojosan Summit Route

★ **Rating:** Moderate

⟲ **Route Type:** Loop

⚲ **Distance:** 5 km

🕐 **Duration:** 3–4 hr

⛰ **Elevation Gain:** 400 m

🛒 **Stroller Friendly:** No

🚩 **GPS START:** 34.783683, 128.632291 (at the parking lot)

🔺 **GPS SUMMIT:** 34.784405, 128.616165 (at Nojosan summit at 565 m)

🚩 **GPS FINISH:** 34.783683, 128.632291

 ## HIKE DESCRIPTION

Nojosan is the third-highest peak on Geoje Island and offers great views over the entire southern half of the island. Beginning at the parking lot, follow the road walking toward Hakdong (toward the southeast) for about 75 meters until you see a wooden staircase on the right-hand side and a trail sign that points toward the summit. The trail enters the forest and begins to gain elevation quickly. There are fiber mats on the trail to prevent excessive damage by overuse or heavy rainfall. Along the route, you'll find several benches. After about 1.3 kilometers, the trail will split, at which point you'll go right to take the trail to the summit.

The path will level out for a little while before beginning to climb along a rocky trail up to a ridgeline where it will intersect with another trail. Turn right and hike a short distance through a tunnel of bushes. The trail will suddenly open up onto a clearing where the summit marker neatly crowns a rocky bald with a fire lookout post, radio antenna, and a helipad nearby. You'll find ample room

to stretch out and enjoy the sun while taking in the views that stretch out in all directions from this commanding height.

Once you're rested, backtrack along the ridgeline trail, passing the intersection trail you used to reach the summit. Continue following the ridgeline, bearing to the south until you reach a two-story pagoda-style gazebo shelter. At the gazebo you have a choice to continue along the ridgeline toward Garasan, the highest mountain on Geoje. This spectacular ridgeline hike is known as the "Jagged Ridge" for many reasons! (See Hike 86 for more details.) However, for this hike, you will take the alternate trail and bear downhill to your left, heading back to the parking lot.

Nojosan Summit Route

Nojosan
565m

P Start

Gazebo

To Garasan via "Jagged Ridge" Route

0   500m

N

Hike 83 MODERATE

Garasan Summit Loop

- ★ **Rating:** Moderate
- 🔄 **Route Type:** Loop
- 📍 **Distance:** 8.5 km
- 🕐 **Duration:** 5–6 hr
- ⛰ **Elevation Gain:** 530 m
- 🚼 **Stroller Friendly:** No

🚩 **GPS START:** 34.729993, 128.613169 (at the parking area adjacent to an old petrol station)

▲ **GPS SUMMIT:** 34.754224, 128.622031 (at Garasan summit at 585 m)

🚩 **GPS FINISH:** 34.729993, 128.613169

📖 HIKE DESCRIPTION

At 585 meters, Garasan is the highest mountain on Geoje Island, with fantastic views of the surrounding area. The variety of terrain, wide panoramas, and well-marked ruins of a 500-year-old fortress are a few other highlights of this hike. Note that there are no views from the forested summit, but there are plenty of other views along the way.

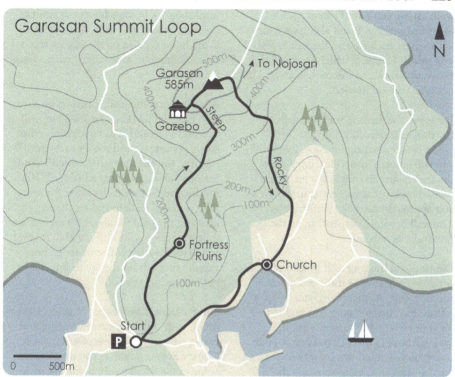

Garasan Summit Loop

The hike starts at a defunct petrol station parking lot at the junction of three roads, referred to as the "3-Way Junction" on some trail markers. Walk about 175 meters along the road, heading east until you reach a short clearing and 50-meter dirt road on your left-hand side. Cross the main road and hike up this short dirt road until the trail comes into view on your right.

The trail is steep and advances quickly up the mountain, levels off briefly, and continues going up. At the top of this second upslope, look for the ruins. Soon enough you will cross a circular stone wall several meters high and thick. Tree roots are entwined in the rocks, and the overgrowth is heavy, but the ruins can still be seen and look similar to a mini (Siem Reap-style) Cambodian temple. As you pass over the stone wall, follow the trail across the top of the fortress ruins until you reach the other side of the fortress wall. There, you'll find a bench and historical marker. You'll also have a view of the sheer rock face on the southwesterly side of Garasan, which looms high above and about 1.5 kilometers away. This is where you are headed.

Pass over the fortress wall and follow the trail as it descends into the thick forest before starting upslope. Eventually you will emerge into a clearing where the trail bears sharply to the left. Soon, several rocky expanses come into view as you approach the rocky cliff from below. The trail becomes serpentine, so use the handrails as needed.

Continue up the trail as it becomes progressively steeper until you reach the ridgeline. At this point, you will join a trail that runs to your right and left. To your right is the summit, but first you will bear to the left, passing over an overgrown helipad toward a two-story gazebo shelter. When you reach the shelter, you'll find one of the best views in Geoje, and the open ground and rocky ledge are perfect for taking a rest as the seabirds wheel overhead, riding the thermals. The views are expansive over the island and far out to sea, where dozens of small rocky islets make up part of the Hallyeo Haesang National (Maritime) Park. Far below lies the village of Dadae with its small white houses with orange metal roofs, blue water tanks, and a white church bell tower.

Once you have reveled in nature's wonders, proceed back across the overgrown helipad to the junction, passing the trail you took to the ridgeline. Instead of taking it, go straight toward the summit of Garasan. The trail will descend slightly and then rise and pass through some low rock wall ruins, then you will suddenly emerge onto a large open field that offers expansive views in all directions. Continue across this grassy bald and stay on the trail for 25 meters more

until the rock marker for the summit of Garasan comes into view. Although this is the highest point on the island, it is a bit anticlimactic, since there are no views from here.

After bagging the peak, proceed on the trail past the marker, and soon you will descend to a sandy bald with high grass. At this point you will see a nearby trail running toward the north, which would take you along the "Jagged Ridge" (Hike 86) toward Nojosan. However, for this hike, you will walk to the southeast, crossing the bald for about 50 meters and following the various hiking club markers to the trail, which will start to descend rapidly through light-growth forest and get increasingly rocky.

Not far from the entrance of this trail and off on your right is a natural spring and creek, where small pools of water form. The creek gets larger as you descend. In some of the small pools, if you are lucky, you may see freshwater crayfish the size of a large coin.

Continuing down the mountain, the trail becomes very rocky and the trees crowd out all views. Be careful not to slip on the wet, loose stones, and stay on the trail. Soon, a fence will indicate civilization is near, and some small farm plots will come into view as you pass out of the forest and emerge onto a concrete farm road. Follow the road as it passes fields and a small creek, which leads toward the ocean and the village of Dadae.

Following the creek, you will pass through Dadae and join the main road adjacent to the two-story church that you sighted from far atop the mountain. Now, facing the harbor across the main road, turn to the left and follow the main road for about 1.6 kilometers until you emerge at the top of a rise and see (about 200 meters away) the parking lot where you began the hike.

Hike 84 `MODERATE`

Mangsan Summit Loop

⭐ **Rating:** Moderate

🔄 **Route Type:** Loop

📍 **Distance:** 8 km

🕐 **Duration:** 5 hr

🏔 **Elevation Gain:** 390 m

🛺 **Stroller Friendly:** No

🚩 **GPS START:** 34.726008, 128.603156 (at the Myeongsa Beach parking lot)

🔺 **GPS SUMMIT:** 34.714041, 128.601316 (at Mangsan summit at 397 m)

🏁 **GPS FINISH:** 34.726008, 128.603156

 ## HIKE DESCRIPTION

Mangsan is the southernmost mountain of the "11 Famous Peaks of Geoje," and it is also one of the smallest of the peaks. However, for what it lacks in elevation it more than makes up for in raw beauty, rugged nature, and truly inspirational ocean views! This is a very popular hike, and it is not uncommon to see a few coaches full of tourists enjoying this scenic loop on the weekends.

You will start this hike in the seaside village of Myeongsa Beach at the large beachfront parking lot. From the parking lot, look to the northeast, where Garasan's 585-meter rocky peak looms over the entire southern half of the island. Turn to the south and follow

the eastern edge of the parking lot road, passing the elementary school on your left. Continue for about 125 meters and pass through the village until you reach the main road. At the road, turn right and proceed for about 300 meters until you see the trailhead and a signboard across the road. Cross the road and take the trail up into the woods.

The trail climbs steeply, and after about 10 minutes, a rocky outcrop offers a good place to rest catch some views. Stay on the trail and continue the steep ascent up toward the ridgeline. There, you will come to the first rocky bald, which has a small green fire watch shelter atop it. But do not stop here; instead, press on for a another 40 meters to the rocky peak and summit marker for Mangsan.

From the rocky summit, you have unobstructed views in nearly all directions, and to the south, you'll see many small islands. After soaking in the sun and sea breezes, continue on the trail as it dips down before climbing a bit and crossing a small stairway and bridge. Look back at the summit and marvel at its beauty and at how far you have already descended. This hike will test you time and again

as you climb up one rocky peak after another, constantly gaining and losing elevation.

Staying on the trail, you will soon emerge at a pile of large boulders surrounded by trees and a lovely view over the ocean. As you arc around the ridgeline, the trail turns from the easterly direction more to the north, and a large staircase will come into view. Before descending the stairs, back up a few meters and take a short spur trail about 10 meters to the south, which leads to a rock outcrop with more amazing views. Return to the staircase and climb down it, staying on the trail as the route descends and then rises again through thick forest in a northerly direction. Eventually, after passing one smaller rocky rise offering views to the northeast toward Dadae Village, descend to the three-way junction where the trail ends at the main road. **(Note: A WC is located here.)**

At the road junction, turn to the left and follow the road bearing downhill, passing the old petrol station on your right. After 300 meters, take your first right and turn onto the paved road that descends down to the harbor as it passes vegetable fields on the right and left. In the autumn you may see piles of cabbage being harvested and prepped for kimchee. At the end of the road, squeeze between a few buildings and emerge in the town square opposite the local ferry terminal. Turn to your left and follow the road as it winds along the edge of the harbor on your right, and follow the road for 1 kilometer until you reach the parking lot where you began the hike.

Note: From the harbor front, you will have a clear view of Garasan, the highest peak on Geoje.

Hike 85 DIFFICULT

Mundong Falls to Okneyobong Summit Loop

⭐ **Rating:** Difficult

🔁 **Route Type:** Loop

📍 **Distance:** 11.5 km

🕐 **Duration:** 6–8 hr

⛰️ **Elevation Gain:** 750 m

🛒 **Stroller Friendly:** No

🚩 **GPS START:** 34.856649, 128.659749 (at the parking lot)

🔺 **GPS SUMMIT:** 34.852308, 128.693446 (at Okneyobong summit at 554.7 m)

🏁 **GPS FINISH:** 34.856649, 128.659749

 ## HIKE DESCRIPTION

This day hike takes in the largest waterfall on Geoje and the island's fourth-highest peak, which towers above Okpo and DSME Shipyard. You will start as in Hike 72 at the Mundong Falls parking lot and proceed to the falls. At the falls, cross the bridge below and continue on the trail as it winds up and around the falls to the left, until you come to a four-way junction with a small shelter. At the junction, turn right and follow the trail as it passes through heavy forest, making sure to stay on the main trail and follow signs for Okneyobong summit. After the trail takes a sharp turn from a southbound direction to the east, a gazebo shelter will come into view. From this vantage point, you will see Jisepo and across the southern foothills.

Staying on the trail, you will soon emerge into a grassy field and pass a trail on your left that descends to Aju-dong. For now, stay straight and start the final push up to the top of Okneyobong. Once at the summit, enjoy the views and a well-earned rest!

Backtrack down to the grassy field junction and turn right to descend the trail toward Aju-dong. This trail will cross a large, well-defined fire road after about 300 meters and a 100-meter elevation drop. At this fire road, turn left. Follow the contours of the northern slope of the mountain and descend slowly through the forest. Stay on the fire road as it zigzags all the way down to the head of the Aju-dong Valley, and soon you will see the tops of massive apartment towers. Stay on the road as it changes from dirt to concrete, following signs for Mundong Falls. After climbing a good 100 meters in elevation, you will emerge at the four-way junction with the shelter. From this point, go straight downhill (backtracking on the morning's initial climb) to Mundong Falls and then on to the parking lot where you began the hike.

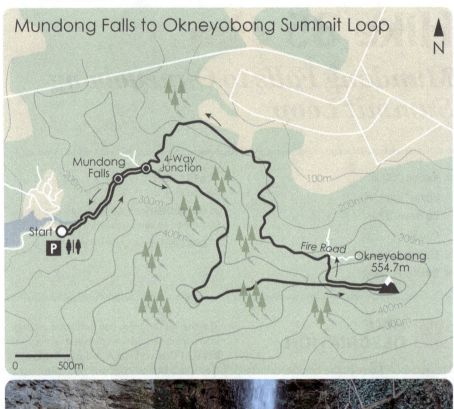

Mundong Falls to Okneyobong Summit Loop

N

Mundong Falls

4-Way Junction

Start

P

Fire Road

Okneyobong 554.7m

100m

200m

300m

300m

400m

400m

300m

200m

0   500m

Hike 86 `DIFFICULT`

Jagged Ridge Route (Nojosan to Garasan)

⭐ **Rating:** Difficult

🔁 **Route Type:** Point to Point

📍 **Distance:** 9.6 km

🕐 **Duration:** 6 hr

🏔 **Elevation Gain:** 800 m

🛒 **Stroller Friendly:** No

🚩 **GPS START:** 34.783683, 128.632291 (at the parking lot)

🔺 **GPS SUMMIT:** 34.784405, 128.616165 (at Nojosan summit at 565 m)

🔺 **GPS SUMMIT:** 34.754224, 128.622031 (at Garasan summit at 585 m)

🚩 **GPS FINISH:** 34.765392, 128.635483 (at the bus stop on Hwy 14, south of Hakdong)

HIKE DESCRIPTION

You can bag two peaks (the highest, Garasan; and third-highest, Nojosan) on this ridgeline hike. The hike offers many rocky outcrops, viewing platforms, and plenty of challenges as the trail rises and drops along the ridgeline, gaining and losing elevation. Ladders and small metal platforms along the rocky ridgeline allow hikers to make their way safely, increasing the excitement value of this route. Since this hike is point to point, you will want to position a second car near the finish or plan on calling a taxi to

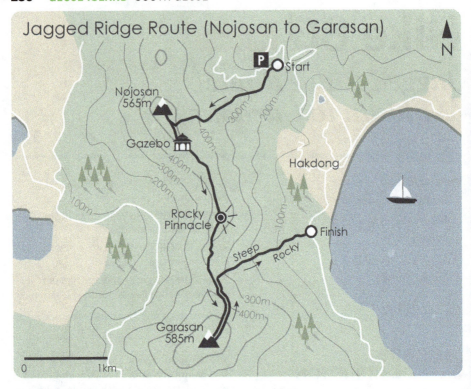

Jagged Ridge Route (Nojosan to Garasan)

pick you up and return you back to the starting point.

You will start this hike at the same location as Hike 82 and follow the same route to the summit of Nojosan. At the gazebo, do not descend but instead follow the trail sign toward Garasan. Follow the ridge, stopping to admire the amazing views from rocky outcrops along the way. About 1 kilometer before you reach the summit of Garasan, you will pass a small shelter on your right that has a trail marker pointing downslope to the left. Don't take this trail, but make note of where it is as you will backtrack to this point after bagging Garasan.

From this point on, the trail begins to climb upslope about 100 meters in elevation until you emerge out of the forest and into a sandy field full of grass. The summit marker for Garasan is 50 meters away to the south in a field of

trees. Follow the trail on the right of the sandy area and you will soon reach the summit. Proceed beyond the summit about 25 meters for fantastic views over the south of the island before backtracking to the shelter.

At this point, follow the trail heading steeply downslope to the east. When I first hiked this trail, I asked a Korean friend of mine what the red Hangul characters on the signpost said, as markers are usually always white. His response was a polite "Don't be scared." In other words, this section needs to be traveled with care! The trail is steep and rocky, and many stones are loose. The descent is about 1.5 kilometers and is quite steep for the first kilometer. Thereafter it becomes easier, and about 450 meters before you reach the finish on the highway you will pass a few small farms. At the highway, take your choice of transport back to Hakdong Village and the start of the hike.

Hike 87 DIFFICULT

Figure 8 Loop

- ★ **Rating:** Difficult
- **Route Type:** Loop
- **Distance:** 16.5 km
- **Duration:** 9–10 hr
- **Elevation Gain:** 1,050 m
- **Stroller Friendly:** No

🚩 **GPS START:** 34.726008, 128.603156 (at the Myeongsa Beach parking lot)

🔺 **GPS SUMMIT:** 34.714041, 128.601316 (at Mangsan summit at 397 m)

🔺 **GPS SUMMIT:** 34.754224, 128.622031 (at Garasan summit at 585 m)

🚩 **GPS FINISH:** 34.726008, 128.603156

📖 HIKE DESCRIPTION

This is a full-day hike that will challenge even the fittest of hikers. This hike is the same as Hike 84 but is then followed by Hike 83. Please see those hikes for a complete hike description. On this hike, you will be able to enjoy ocean views dotted with rocky islands stretching far out to sea, fortress ruins, and both the highest and lowest peaks of the "11 Famous Peaks" of Geoje.

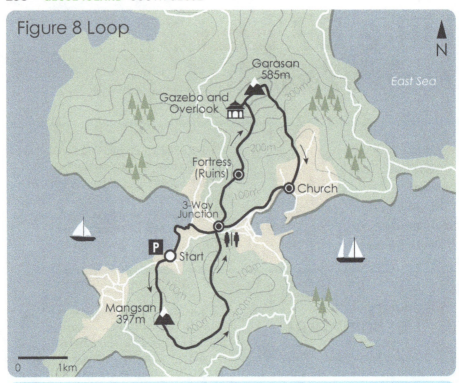

Figure 8 Loop

N

Garasan
585m

Gazebo and
Overlook

East Sea

Fortress
(Ruins)

Church

3-Way
Junction

P   Start

Mangsan
397m

0   1km

Hike 88 VERY DIFFICULT

Blood, Sweat, and Tears Route

★ **Rating:** Very Difficult

⟳ **Route Type:** Point to Point

📍 **Distance:** 26 km

🕐 **Duration:** 10–12 hr

⛰ **Elevation Gain:** 1,450 m

👶 **Stroller Friendly:** No

◥ **GPS START:** 34.830446, 128.655009 (at the parking lot at Simwonsa Temple)

▲ **GPS SUMMIT:** 34.822537, 128.656575 (at Bookbyeongsan summit at 465.4 m)

▲ **GPS SUMMIT:** 34.784405, 128.616165 (at Nojosan summit at 565 m)

▲ **GPS SUMMIT:** 34.754224, 128.622031 (at Garasan summit at 585 m)

▲ **GPS SUMMIT:** 34.714041, 128.601316 (at Mangsan summit at 397 m)

⚑ **GPS FINISH:** 34.726008, 128.603156 (at the Myeongsa Beach parking lot)

 ## HIKE DESCRIPTION

This ridgeline hike allows peak baggers to bag four of the "11 Famous Peaks of Geoje" while taking in the most scenic and rugged part of Geoje Island. The trail snakes from north to south along the island's main mountain range, over rocky ridgelines and through deep forests, en route to Myeongsa Beach at the southern terminus.

This hike is a combination of the following: 1) Hike 81, 2) Hike 86, 3) Hike 83 (in reverse starting from the Garasan summit to the three-way junction), and 4) Hike 84 (in reverse from the three-way junction to the Mangsan summit to the finish point at Myeongsa Beach). Study the above routes before attempting this one.

The only trail not covered earlier in this guidebook follows a ridgeline through thick, undulating forests. This part of the trail links the terminus of Hike 81 to the beginning of Hike 86. This particular stretch starts right across the road from where you finish Hike 81, where you'll see a large trail sign at the trailhead. **(Note: There is a short spur trail just off to your left at an outcrop known as "Big Rock" that offers views over the bay and Gujora Beach.)**

Follow the main trail as it makes its way through the forest, offering occasional views to the east and west. Eventually you will pass a large radio tower on your right-hand side. From this point, you have only about 2.8 kilometers remaining before you reach the mountain pass road, which crosses the mountain range from Hakdong Beach heading inland. This is where the next stretch of the trail begins for Nojosan (see Hike 86).

As you approach the mountain pass roadway, pay attention to the mushroom farms in the area. (Sometimes you will see the pine tree logs drilled and prepped with spore plugs to grow mushrooms.)

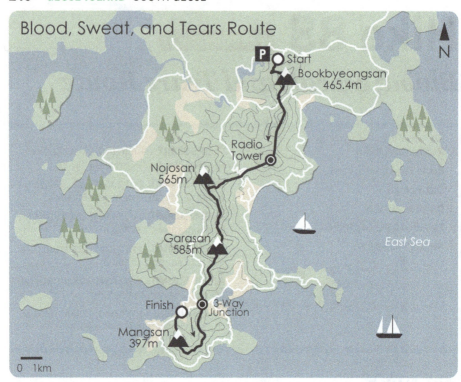

Blood, Sweat, and Tears Route

N

P 🅿 ○ Start
🏔 Bookbyeongsan
465.4m

Radio
Tower ◉

Nojosan
565m 🏔

Garasan
585m 🏔

East Sea

Finish ○ ◉ 3-Way
Junction

Mangsan
397m 🏔

0 1km

Also stop to admire the small graveyard with small Buddhist statues on your left just as you reach the roadway.

Continuing on, follow the route to Nojosan (see Hike 86) and then along the ridgeline to Garasan. However, as noted previously, from the Hike 86 terminus of Garasan, DO NOT backtrack, but instead follow Hike 83 in reverse from the summit of Garasan down to the fortress ruins, and finish at the "3-way junction." Across the road is a WC and the start of the final leg of this epic hike, the Mangsan circuit, in reverse, per Hike 84. Follow the trail all the way to the finish at the beach.

저구삼거리 9.1km →
Jeogu Samgeori(3-way jn.)

가 라 산 4.9km →
Garasan(Mt.)

Glossary
Useful Phrases

Korea has one of the most educated populations in the industrialized world. Many have learned English as a second language, especially those under 40 years of age. Given the presence of American military forces across the ROK and the trading status of the nation, English is commonly spoken, such that usually someone will be able to help you on the trail. That being said, it's always helpful to know some Korean for making friends and getting things done in more rural areas where there may be fewer English speakers around. The list below is a selection of useful and commonly heard/used words in Korea as related to traveling and hiking. It's worth noting that the words pertaining to political, geographical, and cultural features are often used as a suffix at the end of words.

Political Terminology:
도 do – Province
군 gun – County
시 si – City
구 gu – Ward in a city
동 dong – Neighborhood in a city
면 myeon – Rural district
읍 eup – Town
리 ri / ni – Village
마을 maeul – Tourist village

Geographical Features:
산 san – Mountain
봉 bong – Peak
바위 bawi – Rock
골 gol – Valley
강 gang – River
시내 shinae – Stream
폭포 pokpo – Waterfall
동굴 donggul – Cave

National and Provincial Parks:
국립 공원 gukrim gongwon – National park
도립 공원 dorim gongwon – Provincial park
표 pyo – Ticket
사 sa – Temple
암자 amja – Hermitage
가신 gashin – Trail
대피소 daepiso – Shelter
주차장 juchajang – Parking lot
다리 dari – Bridge
성 seong – Mountain fortress

Giving or Seeking Directions:
북 buk – North
동 dong – East
남 nam – South
서 seo – West
우측 ucheuk – Turn right
좌측 jwacheuk – Turn left
오르막 oreumak – Go up
내리막 naerimak – Go down
직진 jikjin – Go straight

Warnings and Help:
정지 jeongji – Stop
주의 juui – Caution
위험 wiheom – Danger
도움 doum – Help
의사 uisa – Doctor
경찰 gyeongchal – Police
잃어버린 ilh-eobeolin – Lost
뱀 baem – Snake
귀찮은 녀석 tik – Tick
개 gae – Dog
물린 mullin – Bitten
응급 처치 eung-geub cheochi – First aid

To/From and Around:
택시 taekshi – Taxi
버스 beosu – Bus
얼마나 eolmana – How much?
얼마나 멀리 eolmana meolli – How far?
얼마나 오래 eolmana olae – How long?

Eating and Drinking:
호텔 hotel – Hotel
식당 shikdang – Restaurant
배고픈 baegopeun – Hungry
물기 없는 mulgi eobsneun – Thirsty
불고기 bulgogi – Marinated beef or pork either grilled or stir-fried
갈비탕 galbitang – Beef rib soup with veggies
파전 pajeon – Panfried vegetable pancake with scallions
김치 kimchee – Fermented spicy cabbage
밥 bap – Rice

라면 ramyeon – Thin refried instant noodles in broth
우동 udong – Thick noodles in broth
짜릿한 jjalishan – Spicy
뜨거운 tteugeoun – Hot
감기 gamgi – Cold
두부 dubu – Bean curd
소주 soju – Rice liquor
막걸리 makgeolli – Rice wine
맥주 maegju – Beer
물 mul – Water
건배 gumbae – Cheers!

Words Commonly Used on the Trail:
안녕하세 annyeonghaseyo — Hello
부디 budi – Please
고맙습니다 gomabseubnida – Thank you
영어 yeongeo – English
지도 jido – Map
비 bi – Rain
스노 sino – Snow
얼음 eol-eum – Ice
흐린 heulin – Muddy
불안정한 bul-anjeonghan – Rocky
미끄러운 mikkeuleoun – Slippery
험한 heomhan – Steep
갑시다 kapshida (or a more familiar form 가자 "Kaja!") – Let's go!

244 FOR FURTHER READING

For Further Reading

Hiking and Camping:
Brown, Ian, and Elizabeth Humphries, eds. *Paddy Pallin's Bushwalking and Camping.* Sydney: Paddy Pallin Pty Ltd., 1995.

Shepard, Roger, Andrew Douch, and David A. Mason. *Baekdu Daegan Trail: Hiking Korea's Mountain Spine.* Seoul: Seoul Selection, 2010.

Korean History and Culture:
Hoare, James, and Geoffrey Chesler, eds. *The Essential Guide to Customs and Culture, Culture Smart! Korea.* London: Kuperard, 2002.

Nahm, Andrew C. *A Panorama of 5000 Years: Korean History.* South Korea: Hollym, 1989.

Quarrington, Dale. *Korean Temples: Art, Architecture and History.* South Korea: CreateSpace Independent Publishing Platform, 2016.

Turnbull, Stephen. *Japanese Castles in Korea 1592–98.* Oxford: Osprey, 2007.

Korean Language:
Jones, B. J., and Gene S. Rhie, eds. *Standard English-Korean, Korean-English Dictionary for Foreigners.* Hollym, 1995.

Korean Phrase Book. Oxford: Berlitz, 1994.

Korean Sightseeing and Cuisine:
Korea Travel Guide. Seoul: Korea Tourism Organization, 2012.

Korean Cuisine. Seoul: Korea Tourism Organization, 2011.

Geoje Island General Information:
Samsung Design and Communications. *Geoje Tourist Resources.* Busan: Geoje City Government, 2010.

Index

About the Author

Erik Palin is a native of Cape Cod, Massachusetts and currently resides in Alaska. He never hiked before Korea and hadn't even seen a hill until he was 14 (on a Boy Scout trip to Vermont). Erik spent over 8 years in the ROK and over 20 in Asia as an expatriate in the maritime and offshore oil and gas industries. He is married to the love of his life, Jozefina, and has four loving daughters who all enjoy hiking. Some of Erik's favorite places to hike include Korea, Japan, Taiwan, Nepal, the Sierra Nevada of California, the South Island of New Zealand, the High Tatras of Slovakia, the Chugach Range of Alaska, and the entire island of Tasmania. He can't wait to discover more trails in new high places and hopes to keep doing this for many, many years to come! Learn more about Erik and his latest adventures at erikpalin.com.

Printed in the USA
CPSIA information can be obtained
at www.ICGtesting.com
LVHW021728220224
772594LV00009B/533